MW01519822

Instructor's Manual and Test Bank
for
Friedman and Schustack

Personality
Classic Theories and Modern Research

Prepared by

Leslie R. Martin
La Sierra University

Howard S. Friedman
University of California, Riverside

Miriam W. Schustack
California State University, San Marcos

Allyn & Bacon
Boston • London • Toronto • Sydney • Tokyo • Singapore

A Viacom Company
160 Gould Street
Needham Heights, Massachusetts 02194

Visit our Web Gallery at http://www.abacon.com for related and support materials.

ISBN 0-205-29316-6

Printed in the United States of America

10 9 8 7 6 5 4 3 2 1 01 00 99 98

TABLE OF CONTENTS

INSTRUCTOR'S MANUAL

TEST BANK

PREFACE

This instructor's supplement has been created to accompany Friedman and Schustack's Personality: Classic Theories and Modern Research. The textbook provides a comprehensive overview of the field of personality psychology, written in an engaging style that has been shown to appeal to and educate students. The textbook is organized into three major parts--an introduction to the definition of personality and the tools for studying it; eight basic theoretical frameworks for understanding personality; and a unique section on applications to individual differences. There is also a concluding chapter which sums up the high points and looks to the future of personality. The preface to the textbook gives a more detailed overview of the structure, approach, and goals of the book.

The instructor's manual provides you, the professor, with a variety of creative ideas for use in your classroom or laboratory (such as discussion topics, individual and class projects, and suggestions of films and videos to complement lecture material).

There is one chapter in this instructor's manual for each chapter in the textbook. Each chapter in this manual is organized as follows:

1. Overview. This section provides a brief overview with suggestions about how to present this chapter.
2. Possible Lecture Outline. This is a brief outline of the major topics in the chapter. This may be used as lecture notes by the instructor, or may be copied as a student handout (some students seem to appreciate an outline to "follow along" with).
3. Classroom Activities, Discussion Topics, and Projects. This section provides activities and questions that might be used to spark discussions or to enrich lectures. Some of the questions may be modified for use as additional essay questions. In addition, ideas for in-class and out-of-class projects are presented; some of the projects are individual in nature, some are for small groups, and some work well with large groups. These projects may be used as homework assignments, or may be used as ungraded class activities to enrich the classroom experience.
4. Recommended Outside Readings. This list suggests several readings for each chapter which should be intriguing to students or professors. Some readings take students "back to the source." Other readings look at a portion of the chapter in more depth, or provide fuel for classroom discussions. Assigning different readings to small groups of students and having them present their findings to the rest of the class is also effective.
5. Films / Videos. At least two films or videos are suggested to accompany each chapter, and a brief description accompanies each. Most are produced for educational use, but a few popular movies have also been included which have been found to stimulate lively conversation. These might be assigned for students to watch on their own time if you do not wish to devote time during class; you may find that most of your students have already seen some of the movies and are happy to offer their opinions and thoughts about them.

In the middle of this manual (before the test bank chapters) you will find two **sample syllabi** (one for a semester-long class and one for a quarter -long class) and two "**projects**" which might be used as alternatives to the traditional term paper. Each of these projects is more involved than any of the projects presented in the chapters and should be assigned early in the quarter/semester; it is helpful if students are allowed to turn in at least one rough draft during the term.

The Test Bank section is also divided into fifteen chapters, with each chapter providing a set of test questions appropriate to the corresponding chapter in the textbook. The test questions in each chapter are organized into two sections:

1. **Multiple Choice Questions**. Multiple choice questions are based on the information presented in the chapter; some questions are factual (definitions, recognition) and others are conceptual (student has to apply knowledge or make an inference to answer the question). Each question has five answer options. Questions are characterized as to their difficulty level: 'E' for 'Easy', 'M' for 'Medium', and 'C' for 'Challenging. Humor is sometimes sneaked in to the answer options, to keep students calm and motivated during a long exam.
2. **Essay Questions**. The essay questions vary in difficulty as well; some essay questions might more accurately be termed "short answer" while others require significant thought and integration.

Personality psychology should not be some dry academic exercise or historical curiosity. Rather, as is maintained throughout the textbook, the study of personality goes to the basis of what it means to be a person.

Leslie R. Martin, Ph.D.,
Howard S. Friedman, Ph.D., &
Miriam W. Schustack, Ph.D.

Your comments and feedback on the textbook or this Instructor's Manual will be greatly appreciated and will be considered during revisions.

Professor Leslie Martin
Psychology Department
La Sierra University,
4700 Pierce Street
Riverside, CA 92515.
lmartin@LaSierra.edu

Professor Howard Friedman
Psychology Department
University of California
Riverside, CA 92521
friedman@citrus.ucr.edu

Professor Miriam Schustack
Psychology Department
California State University
San Marcos, CA 92096
mschusta@csusm.edu

Professor Leslie Martin teaches psychology at La Sierra University and has successfully used an early draft of Personality: Classic Theories and Modern Research to teach personality psychology. She received her Ph.D. from the University of California, Riverside.

Professor Howard S. Friedman teaches psychology at the University of California, Riverside, where he currently studies personality and health. In 1995, Dr. Friedman was awarded UCR's Distinguished Teaching Award. He is an elected Fellow of the Division of Personality and Social Psychology, and the Division of Health Psychology, of the American Psychological Association. An honors graduate of Yale University, Friedman received his Ph.D. from Harvard University.

Professor Miriam W. Schustack teaches psychology at the California State University in San Marcos (near San Diego), where she currently specializes in the use of computers in learning. She previously taught at Harvard University. An honors graduate of Princeton University, Schustack received her master's from Yale and her Ph.D. from Carnegie-Mellon University.

CHAPTER 1: WHAT IS PERSONALITY?

This chapter introduces the field of personality by explaining the distinctive orientations of the field, its history and origins, its basic approaches, and some key recurring issues, such as personal versus situational influences. Consistent with the whole approach of the text, it builds up from examples and concepts that students can readily comprehend.

Most students come to the study of personality eager to understand themselves and others. It is valuable to build upon their interests and gradually lead them to grasp and employ the sophisticated and rigorous concepts and methods of personality psychology. Relating theories back to real-life examples helps students understand, retain, and appreciate the material.

Possible Lecture Outline

I. The basic question that personality psychologists seek to answer is, "What makes us unique-- what makes us a human being?"

II. Personality psychology is the scientific study of psychological forces.
   A. Unconscious
   B. Ego forces
   C. Cognitive
   D. Biological
   E. Conditioning/shaping
   F. Traits/skills
   G. Spiritual/existential
   H. Person-situation interaction

III. Because personality psychologists use scientific methods to test their theories, conclusions are much more reliable and valid (compared to those obtained from astrology, palm-reading, physiognomy, etc.).
   A. Importance of data and statistics for scientific testing of many theories
   B. Distinction between correlation and causation

IV. What are the sources of personality theories?
   A. Careful observation and deep introspection of insightful thinkers
   B. Systematic empirical research
   C. Concepts borrowed from other disciplines (note that knowledge gleaned from other disciplines may also be used to test present theories-- for instance, if new advances in biochemistry show that one theory of personality is impossible, the theory must then be reworked to be consistent with current biochemical

knowledge).
D. Most theories utilize some aspect of all three of these

V. Preview of perspectives
A. Psychoanalytic
B. Neo-analytic
C. Cognitive
D. Biological
E. Behaviorist
F. Trait/Skill
G. Humanistic/Existential
H. Person-Situation Interactionist

VI. Brief history of personality psychology
A. Theater & self-presentation
B. Religious influences
C. Evolutionary biology
D. Progression of testing

VII. Modern theory
A. Allport: The search for underlying organizational properties, and a focus on individuality.
B. Lewin: Gestalt tradition, integrative nature of perception and thought, a whole that is greater than the sum of the parts; believed in the importance of changing situations.
C. Murray: Emphasis on comprehensive orientation-- longitudinal design; personology.
D. M. Mead: Highlighted the importance of cross-cultural comparisons.

VIII. Issues to be addressed throughout the course
A. The importance of the unconscious?
B. The definition of the self
C. Unique vs. general approaches to studying people
D. Male-female differences
E. Personal vs. situational influences
F. Cultural determinants of personality
G. Usefulness of personality for understanding behavior

Classroom Activities, Discussion Topics, and Projects

1. Ask students to define, in one paragraph, what is meant by the term "personality." Students should be thorough yet precise. Have students read these paragraphs aloud and focus in on the major points that are generally seen as important by students. Have students save these paragraphs for comparison to each of the perspectives described in the book.

2. Have students describe themselves in a paragraph. Identify how much of what they say about themselves is personality-related and how much relates only to social roles and accomplishments. Discuss how these areas overlap and what distinguishes them.

3. What were some of the most important early impacts and biases on personality study? Biological understanding of the times? Gender-related beliefs of the times? Religious beliefs and superstitions? What are the important influences today? Gender issues? Cross-cultural issues? New innovations in physiological measurement?

4. Have students write down and pass in questions they have about personality. (They may say things like, "Why are men like my boyfriend so aggressive and untrustworthy in love?") Answer the questions, as appropriate, in lectures throughout the course. (Shows the "relevance" of the course.)

5. Have students write down a one-sentence description of each of the eight basic perspectives to be covered in the course (this works best if this is the first class period and the students have not yet read the introductory chapter). Have students share their responses before going briefly over the eight perspectives. Collect the student responses and save them to hand back at the end of the quarter/semester (students are often surprised to see how much they have learned).

Recommended Outside Readings

Loevinger, J. (1987). Paradigms of personality (pp. 1-5; Study of personality as science). New York: W.H. Freeman & Company.

Gadlin, H. & Ingle, G. (1975). Through the one-way mirror; The limits of experimental self-reflection. American Psychologist, 30, 1003-1009.

Craik, K., Hogan, R. & Wolfe, R. (1993). Fifty years of personality psychology. NY: Plenum.

Films / Videos

"Landmarks in Psychology." A good introduction to some of the big names in personality psychology; presented in a slide-show format. Outlines some major approaches to personality (interpersonal, humanistic, behavioral existential). 50 minutes. Insight Media: 212-721-6316. 1980.

"Personality." Looks at psychoanalytic, behavioral, cognitive, humanistic, and trait approaches to personality; also addresses a bit of current research in personality (made in 1990 so doesn't have all the latest stuff). 30 minutes. Insight Media. 1990.

CHAPTER 2: HOW IS PERSONALITY STUDIED AND ASSESSED?

This chapter first explains the importance of careful measurement, and it goes on to talk about reliability and validity. Response sets and other biases are explained. This chapter then describes ten basic types of assessment, with examples.

Instructors who spend more time on measurement issues or psychotherapeutic issues can complement this chapter with more material in lectures or discussion sections, since it is written and organized in an open, clear, and simple structure. At the other extreme, instructors who take a more "theories" approach can safely move quickly through this material.

Too many students are turned off (unnecessarily) by issues of measurement and statistics. Students are fascinated, however, when they see assessment as a tool to measure things that they are interested in measuring (such as precisely what makes someone charismatic). Remember also that the "Self Understanding" boxes in chapters 3 - 14 provide additional examples of personality assessment, relevant to students' lives.

Possible Lecture Outline

I. What is subjective assessment? Measurement that relies on interpretation.
   - A. Problems with subjective assessment: Judges may not agree in their judgments; even when they do agree, they may still be wrong.
   - B. Advantages of subjective assessment. Complex phenomena may be examined and valuable insights gained.

II. What is reliability? Consistency in scores or ratings that are expected to be consistent. Random variations in measurement are called "error of measurement" or "error variance." What about different ways of assessing reliability?
   - A. Internal consistency and split-half reliability
   - B. Cronbach's coefficient alpha for internal consistency
   - C. Test-retest reliability (measure of consistency over time)

III. But what happens when people change? When our environments influence us in different ways? How can we then have "reliable" personality assessments?
   - A. Look at personality as an underlying influence that affects behavior-- that is, specific responses or behaviors might change over time, but consistent underlying patterns should be discernible.
   - B. Look for consistency in the short term, but expect changes when looking over periods of many years. Also, expect to see some changes after life-changing transitions and/or traumatic events.

IV. What is validity? Are we measuring what we think we are measuring? Construct validity is ascertained by finding whether behaviors, attitudes, etc. that are theoretically relevant to the construct can be predicted by the measure.

A. Convergent validity: a measure is related to what it should be related to
B. Discriminant validity: a measure is not related to what it should not be related to
C. Criterion-related validity: the measure can predict important outcome criteria
D. Content validity: the measure accurately measures the domain it is supposed to
E. Because proper test validation requires the establishment of several different types of validity, and the assessment of various traits, it is called "multitrait-multimethod"

V. How does one choose items to include in a personality test?

A. Items should discriminate among individuals with varying levels of the measured trait
B. Items should be inter-correlated, but not so highly that they are overly redundant
C. The final assessment should have a normal distribution (individuals very high or very low, as well as in the middle, should be measurable with the test)

VI. The problem of response sets and what to do about them

A. Some items should be reverse-coded to avoid the "acquiescence response set"
B. Items should be worded as neutrally as possible to avoid the "social desirability response set"
C. Lie scales may be used to pick up random response patterns, or those who are lying
D. It's best to use several different methods of assessment, since none is without bias

VII. What about the problem of biases in psychological testing? All tests must make assumptions about the background, knowledge, and abilities of the person taking the test. Some of these assumptions will be incorrect. This doesn't mean the tests shouldn't be used, it just means that we must be careful in our interpretations, and look at the context to which results are applied.

A. Ethnic bias is one of the most common forms of bias-- a characteristic that may be a strength is one culture is perceived as a weakness or deficiency in another
B. Gender bias is also common-- characteristics that are strengths for one group, or that are simply not socialized for one group, are perceived as weaknesses or "missing" for another group

VIII. What are the different kinds of personality tests?

A. Self-report tests; these are usually pencil and paper tests (questionnaires). Some examples include the MMPI, MCMI, NEO-PI, and MBTI

B. Another type of self-report test, which may be more flexible than the traditional questionnaire, is the Q-sort. The individual places cards, each with a descriptive word or term, into piles indicating how characteristic the descriptor is of him or her. The piles are arranged into a forced-normal distribution (that is, only a few of the cards can be placed in the "most characteristic" or "least characteristic" piles).

C. Ratings and judgments; this is when someone else fills out a questionnaire or answers questions about the target (subject)

D. Biological measures; early attempts included phrenology and body-typing, while some more modern variations include things like palm reading. More reliable forms of biological assessment include recording brain waves, levels of brain chemicals, and hormones.

E. Behavioral observations; these include actually watching people perform various behaviors, as well as experience sampling (such as having a person carry a beeper and then write down what he or she is doing each time the beeper goes off)

F. Interviews; these include unstructured interviews (which are more free and thus potentially more rich, but also more difficult to assess in terms of validity) and structured interviews (more valid, but also more likely to miss important individual nuances). In general, interviews of any type are easily biased by the preconceptions and behaviors of the interviewer.

   1. A nice example of a structured interview is that for Type A behavior pattern

G. Expressive behavior; this involves a careful analysis of *how* people do things--how they move or talk, for example-- rather than *what* they do. Expressive style is often biased by cultural and gender-related factors.

H. Document analysis; this technique involves careful analysis of an individual's writings such as letters, diaries, etc. Writings such as these are most useful as supplements to other sources of information, but may be a rich source of data in their own right.

I. Projective tests; these assessment tools require one to draw a picture, complete a sentence, tell a story about an ambiguous stimulus, or interpret an ambiguous stimulus. The goal is to gain access to unconscious motives and concerns, but again there is a lot of room for bias in interpretation.

   1. Some good examples of projective tests include the Rorschach Inkblot Test, the Thematic Apperception Test, and the Draw-A-Person Test.

J. Demographics; this includes gathering information about the person's age, place of birth, religion, family size, etc. Although these variables are not psychological in nature, they can aid in reaching a more complete understanding of the makeup of an individual.

IX. What are some of the ethical issues in personality testing?

A. Test results will always contain some "error" and thus will always be somewhat inaccurate.

B. When these tests are used to identify those who should be excluded from something (like school, medical treatment, etc.) these errors become very important.

C. The fact that errors do occur should not preclude our making use of the psychological assessment tools that are available.

D. Instead, we must be careful at many points in the assessment process

1. In our interpretation of test results
2. When choosing how to apply our knowledge
3. In the construction of new tests,
4. open to revision of "tried and true" measures if new information becomes available).

Classroom Activities, Discussion Topics, and Projects

1. Have students create a "personality test" to measure a single trait. Be sure that they take into account things like acquiescent responding, social desirability, etc. Students can collect data from one another and attempt to establish the various types of reliability. Depending on the time frame available, some form of validity may also be assessed. Discuss the problems students encountered during this scale creation exercise.

2. Discuss historical and contemporary instances in which measures have been abused (particularly psychological measures). How might these situations have been avoided? What can be done to ensure that similar things do not happen in the future?

3. Discuss the relation of theory to measurement-- that is, how is measurement creation influenced by current theory, and how do measures change as theories change or new explanations for phenomena are uncovered?

4. This chapter describes many different ways of assessing personality. Discuss the strengths and weaknesses of each, in comparison with the others. Work in small groups to create a multitrait-multimethod plan for testing a theory or measuring a personality trait or cluster of traits. Discuss these plans in terms of feasibility, bias, etc.

5. Have students answer questions related to "social desirability" [see Crowne, D.P., & Marlowe, D. (1964). *The approval motive: Studies in evaluative dependence.* New York: Wiley]. Discuss the measurement implications of finding a high level of social desirability when administering a psychological test.

6. On a volunteer basis, let each student assess certain aspects of the personality of a fellow student in the class. Of course this is potentially a sensitive matter and needs adequate preparation to protect the rights and safety of each individual. (Should not be supervised solely by Teaching Assistants; needs active involvement of the professor.)

Recommended Outside Readings

Fiske, D. W. (1971). *Measuring the concepts of personality.* Chicago: Aldine.

Gould, S. J. (1981). *The Mismeasure of man.* New York: W. W. Norton.

Campbell, D. T. (1960). Recommendations for the APA test standards regarding construct, trait, and discriminant validity. *American Psychologist,* 15, 546-553.

Tellegen, A. (1991). Personality traits: Issues of definition, evidence, and assessment. In Thinking clearly about psychology: Essays in honor of Paul E. Meehl. Vol. 1: Matters of public interest; Vol. 2: Personality and psychopathology.; Dante Cicchetti & William M. Grove, Eds. Minneapolis: University of Minnesota Press, p. 10-35.

Films / Videos

"Discovering Psychology: Understanding Research." This is Part 2 of a tape in the "Discovering Psychology" series (Part 1 is on the same tape). This half takes about 30 minutes. Provides a general overview of research methods in psychology (not specific to personality). Zimbardo is the "leader." 30 minutes. 1990. Annenberg/CPB Multimedia Collection: 800-532-7637.

"Personality." This is from the Psychology Today series, and looks at how college students' views of self differ from the opinions of their parents and friends. Describes various kinds of personality evaluations. 29 minutes. 1971. PCR: Films and Video in the Behavioral Sciences: 814-865-6314.

CHAPTER 3: PSYCHOANALYTIC ASPECTS

This chapter begins the presentation of the eight basic aspects of personality by discussing Freudian theory and its modern-day counterparts. The theory is seen neither as gospel nor as an archaic relic, but rather as a powerful set of ideas (some true, some false, some still disputed) that significantly influenced 20th century thought.

Students have, of course, heard about Freudian ideas, and they wonder where the mystique comes from. It is perhaps easiest to show the depth and meaning of the ideas by using real-life examples and controversies, such as the phenomenon of "recovered memories" ("recovered" from repression). These are good ways to show both the strengths and weaknesses of a powerful set of ideas. Note also that each chapter has a box on Evaluating the Perspectives (in this case, "*Advantages and Limits of the Psychoanalytic Approach*").

This chapter illustrates Defense Mechanisms with modern-day examples of interest to students. Also distinctive to this chapter is a detailed explanation of how many of the important notions Freud studied are still being studied in modern cognitive psychology. These include Unconscious Motivation, Hypermnesia, Infantile Amnesia, and Subliminal Perception.

Possible Lecture Outline

I. The unconscious
- A. Early in his career Freud began using hypnosis to treat patients
- B. Moved into the realm of suggestion, free-association, and dreams
    1. Dreams called the "royal road" to understanding the unconscious
    2. Manifest vs. latent content (an iceberg is a good analogy)

II. The structure of the mind
- A. Id ("it"): the undifferentiated core of personality; operates according to the pleasure principle
- B. Ego ("I"): the structure which deals with reality; operates according to the reality principle
- C. Superego ("over-I"): the structure which internalizes societal norms; operates according to the morality principle

III. Psychosexual development
  A. Oral Stage--infants satisfy needs primarily through oral means (suckling).
    1. The conflict arises when a child is weaned and must give up the comforting breast.
    2. Difficulty in transferring psychosexual energy (libido) to the next stage results in fixation at the oral stage
      a. may lead to dependency
      b. may lead to preoccupation with oral acquisition (eating, smoking, chewing gum, etc.).
  B. Anal Stage--young children derive pleasure from relieving themselves of bodily waste.
    1. The conflict arises when parents "toilet train" the child--the child may react by refusing to be "trained" or by refusing to relieve him/herself at all.
    2. Difficulty transferring libido to the next stage results in fixation at the anal stage
      a. may lead to excessive usage of bathroom humor
      b. may lead to preoccupation with neatness and order.
  C. Phallic Stage--children gain pleasure from exploring and stimulating their genitals.
    1. The conflict arises because overtly sexual behavior is not socially acceptable.
    2. Oedipus Complex (boys). During this period little boys desire mother and fear that father will punish this desire by castrating them. Resolution requires that little boys transform their fears into admiration and identification.
    3. Electra Complex (girls). During this period little girls wish that they had a penis and blame mother for their inferiority. Resolution requires that little girls identify with mother so that they can obtain a man and have a baby (a penis substitute).
  D. Latency Period. In this period psychosexual energy is channeled into academic and social pursuits.
    1.Because there is no conflict to be resolved, fixation cannot occur.
  E. Genital Stage. In this stage the individual gains satisfaction from mature, heterosexual relationships.
    1. Normal development is characterized by marriage and child-rearing.

IV. Defense mechanisms
   A. Repression: an ego defense mechanism that pushes threatening thoughts/ideas into the unconscious
      1. post-traumatic stress disorder
      2. repressed memories (as with incest); false memories
   B. Reaction formation: an ego defense mechanism that hides threatening impulses by over-emphasizing their opposite in thought and action
      1. the conflicting message and personal action of some televangelists (e.g. Jim Bakker, Jimmy Swaggert)
   C. Denial: an ego defense mechanism which refuses to acknowledge anxiety-provoking stimuli
      1. the sudden death of a loved one
   D. Projection: an ego defense mechanism which attributes anxiety-provoking impulses or thoughts to others
      1. always being suspicious of others and their "selfish motives"
   E. Sublimation: an ego defense mechanism by which dangerous urges are transformed into positive, socially meaningful motivations.
      1. excessive desire to control/dominate others might lead to one to assume leadership roles in the community
   F. Regression: an ego defense mechanism which protects by returning to an earlier, "safer" time of life
      1. distressed individual treating spouse as if s/he were a parent
   G. Rationalization: an ego defense mechanism which creates logical explanations for behaviors which were impulse-driven
      1. a cross-country move to be with a current love-interest is seen as a trip to "find oneself" and "look for new job opportunities"

V. Major Freudian contributions and weaknesses
   A. Contributions
      1. scientific exploration of personality and behavior
      2. emphasis on sexuality in general, and on infant/child sexuality in particular; sexuality as a motivational force
      3. importance of early childhood experience in molding personality
      4. importance of the unconscious
   B. Weaknesses
      1. Freudian theory is very deterministic
      2. derived from study of pathology
      3. difficult to study empirically, to disconfirm
      4. not concerned with lifetime development

VI. Application of psychoanalytic thought
   A. Unconscious emotion and motivation
      1. emotional-motivation states (e.g. anger) can exist independent of thought
      2. some emotions, as expressed facially, are "hard wired" at birth and recognized universally
   B. Hypermnesia ("excess memory")
      1. use of free-association and hypnosis to access memories outside conscious awareness
         a. are they real? certainty doesn't imply accuracy
         b. were they really inaccessible?
      2. rewards and penalties associated with "remembering" have been shown to affect ability to "remember"
   C. Infantile amnesia
      1. young kids "learn" a lot, yet as adults we recall little from prior to age three or four
      2. all memories are "forgotten," not just the traumatic ones
   D. Subliminal perception
      1. we must be able to perceive the message in some part of the brain
      2. a perceived message is quite weak
      3. conscious propaganda is so much more powerful, yet we often overlook its effects
      4. subliminal perception vs. direction of attention
   E. Memory
      1. memories are personalized, rather than duplications of reality
      2. memories change over time
      3. memories vary in their "availability" for conscious recall
      4. explicit vs. implicit memory
   F. Amnesia
      1. behavior may be affected by experiences not "remembered"
      2. evidence for independently operating, unconscious memory systems in the brain

Classroom Activities, Discussion Topics, and Projects

1. Suggest that students "keep a notebook and pen by your bed every night for one week. Each morning when you wake up (or in the night, if a dream awakens you), take a few minutes to write down your dreams in as much detail as you can remember. After a few days you will probably find yourself remembering more details about your dreams than you did on the first day. Use Freudian theory to analyze your dreams. What themes do you see emerging? What symbols do you see? Distinguish between the manifest and latent content of your dreams. Do you think that Freudian theory does a good job of explaining how your dreams reflect your unconscious? If not, what do you think your dreams mean?"

2. Have students think of an interpersonal problem they are currently experiencing (if not a current one, use a past problem). If you asked Freud for help with this problem, what would he say to you? What would he say was the "root" of the problem?

3. Have students identify, if they can, a time when they used each of Freud's ego-defense mechanisms. If they cannot do so for every mechanism, allow them to identify when they have observed someone else using the mechanism. Discuss situations in which ego-defense mechanisms are helpful and times when they might be ultimately harmful

4. Ask students to recall their earliest memory from childhood. Then have them think about why they remember that particular incident.

Recommended Outside Readings

Freud, S. (1963). Three case histories: The "Wolf Man", the "Rat Man", and the psychotic Doctor Schreber. (P. Reiff, Ed.). New York: Macmillan.

Freud, S. (1949). An outline of psychoanalysis. New York: W. W. Norton. (Translated by J. Strachey; originally published in 1940).

Freud, S. (1927) The interpretation of dreams. Translation of 3d ed. with introduction, by A. A. Brill., New York, Macmillan Company.

Brenner, C. (1957). An elementary textbook of psychoanalysis. Garden City, NY: Doubleday.

Masson, J. (1984). The assault on truth: Freud's suppression of the seduction theory. New York: Farrar, Straus, & Giroux.

Sulloway, F. J. (1979). Freud, biologist of the mind: Beyond the psychoanalytic legend. New York: Basic Books.

Films / Videos

"Freud: Hidden Nature of Man." Addresses psychoanalysis, the Oedipal complex, structure of the psyche (id, ego, superego). Format is a dramatized interview with Freud. 29 minutes. 1970. Insight Media: 800-233-9910.

"Sigmund Freud: His Offices and Home." This has pictures from Vienna and makes you feel like you are really there, on a guided tour of Freud's living and working areas. 17 minutes. 1975. FilmMakers Library: 212-808-4980.

"Freud Under Analysis." Discusses Freud's methods of analysis, the unconscious, and Freud's self-analysis. Includes some criticisms of Freudian theory. 58 minutes. 1987. Produced by Nova. Coronet Film & Video: 800-777-8100.

CHAPTER 4: NEO-ANALYTIC AND EGO ASPECTS: IDENTITY

This chapter presents the traditional neo-analytic evolution of Freudian theory (Jung, Adler, Horney, Erikson), but does so with an eye towards modern developments concerning the "self." Jung's main ideas are presented in this chapter but are so wide-ranging that they also pop up elsewhere in this book.

Horney's work is given significant attention, in keeping with this book's desire to embrace a broader perspective. Neo-analysts and object relations theorists (Anna Freud, Heinz Hartman, Robert White, Margaret Mahler, Heinz Kohut, Melanie Klein) are used as a bridge to more modern notions, so that students can appreciate that this work is not some historical curiosity, but rather has led to concepts that are common in our society (competence, attachment/bonding, self-esteem, etc.). Many modern theories of selfhood and life-span development derive from the neo-analytic writings.

Possible Lecture Outline

I. Carl Jung and selfhood
   A. Two themes were prominent in Jung's childhood belief and these were influential in his later theories
      1. He believed that he possessed two different personalities
      2. He believed that his dreams and visions were communications from beyond
   B. Jung divided the psyche into three parts
      1. Ego: the conscious part of personality that embodies sense of self
      2. Personal unconscious: any personal thoughts not currently a part of conscious awareness
      3. Collective unconscious: a deeper level of the unconscious shared with the rest of humanity, and containing archetypes (emotional symbols); the following are just a few archetypes:
         a. animus and anima
         b. persona and shadow
         c. hero and demon
         d. mother
   C. Jung contributed the idea of "complexes" (groups of emotionally-charged, thematic thoughts and feelings) to the field, and developed word association test to study them
   D. Jung believed personality was comprised of opposing forces constantly struggling for dominance and, ideally, resulting in equilibrium
   E. Jung posited four ectopsychic functions and two major attitudes to help describe personality (the intersection of these yields eight possible personality "types")

1. Rational functions: thinking and feeling; irrational functions: sensing and intuiting
2. Attitudes: introversion and extroversion
   a. The Myers-Briggs Type Indicator is a modern personality inventory that is based on Jung's typology

II. Alfred Adler, inferiority complex, and importance of society
  A. Adler was one who believed strongly in the vast complexity of human motivation, as well as the importance of social conditions, as influences on personality
  B. Striving for superiority seen as a central theme of personality-- pervasive feelings of helplessness and inferiority were seen to lead to an "inferiority complex"; in defense, one might develop a "superiority complex"
  C. Adler's theory developed with the following components:
    1. Organ inferiority: everyone is born with a physical weakness; our reactions to these inferiorities motivate life choices
    2. Aggression drive: reaction to perceived inferiority
    3. Masculine protest: striving for independence and competence seen in both boys and girls
    4. Superiority striving: striving to obtain power and superiority over one's own weaknesses and inferiority
    5. Perfection striving: striving to meet fictional goals which goes on indefinitely
  D. Adler believed the following were fundamental social issues every individual must address for him/herself
    1. Occupational tasks: choosing/pursuing fulfilling career
    2. Societal tasks: creating friendships and social networks
    3. Love tasks: finding suitable life-partner
  E. Adler also described personality characteristics typical of first-, second-, last-born, and only children
    1. brought about by the unique social situation into which each is born
  F. Adler's typology combines the four Greek humors with varying levels of social interest and activity level
    1. Ruling-dominant
    2. Getting-leaning
    3. Avoiding
    4. Socially useful

III. Karen Horney, culture, and feminism
  A. Horney rejected Freud's idea of "penis envy", believing instead that envy was based on the independence and power of men's social position
  B. Horney's "basic anxiety" describes a child's fear of being helpless and alone in the world; this internal anxiety could be focused inward or outward; to cope, people adopt one of the following "coping styles"
    1. passive (cope by complying)

2. aggressive (cope by fighting)
3. withdrawn (cope by disengaging)

C. Horney's four aspects of "self"
1. Despised self: feelings of inferiority and shortcomings
2. Real self: inner core of personality
3. Actual self: physical person, apart from outside evaluation
4. Ideal self: what one hopes to become

D. Horney modified her three coping styles in view of how she saw people alienating their real selves
1. "Moving toward" describes those that over-identify with the despised self and strive to please others to get love, affection, and approval
2. "Moving against" describes those that over-identify with the ideal self and are striving for power and control because they feel they deserve it
3. "Moving away" describes those that want to overcome the despised self, but have no hope of achieving the ideal; they withdraw because they feel unworthy of love and don't believe they can become worthy

IV. Other neo-analysts

A. Anna Freud: worked with children as patients and adapted psychoanalytic techniques for them
1. emphasized social influence on the ego

B. Heinz Hartmann: "father of ego psychology"; saw ego as somewhat (but not totally) autonomous-- id and ego were viewed as compensatory

C. Robert White: "freed" the ego from the id; brought ideas of effectance motivation and competence into realm of psychoanalytic thought

V. Object relations theories--focus on the importance of relations with others for defining self

A. Margaret Mahler: her theory of symbiosis described patterns of emotional attachment
1. Normal symbiotic kids formed normal ties
2. Symbiotic psychotic kids formed abnormally strong ties
3. Autistic kids were unable to form ties

B. Melanie Klein: worked with and observed children to discover how they conceptualize others

C. Heinz Kohut: worked with those with narcissistic personality disorder, which he thought grew from a lack of parental acceptance; therapist takes role of accepting parent

VI. Erik Erikson and life span identity

A. Erikson believed that personality development (identity) was <u>not</u>

completed in childhood/adolescence. He posited the following developmental stages (ego crises):

1. Trust vs. mistrust
2. Autonomy vs. shame and doubt
3. Initiative vs. guilt
4. Industry vs. inferiority
5. Identity vs. role confusion
6. Intimacy vs. isolation
7. Generativity vs. stagnation
8. Ego-integrity vs. despair

VII. Modern approaches to identity

A. Modern ego psychologists focus on present identity and future aims, with less emphasis on tracing adult motivations to childhood trauma; they also recognize at least two dimensions of "self": personal and social

B. They are trying to understand what a self-concept is and how it changes (e.g. Cheek, Snyder, Little, Emmons, Cantor, and Baumeister)

Classroom Activities, Discussion Topics, and Projects

1. On a piece of paper write a brief paragraph that describes who you are. Now write another paragraph which describes one of your friends. Compare these two paragraphs. What do your descriptions tell you about the differences between how we view "self" and "others"?

2. Have each student identify his/her position in the birth order of the his/her family. Discuss Adler's beliefs about birth order and predictions about eventual outcomes for individuals who are first-, second-, or last-born (or only-children). Do the students match these profiles? If not, why not? What are some prominent examples (e.g., movie stars, political figures, historical icons) of people who do fit the profiles?

3. Have students list their roles (son/daughter, student, cashier, friend, etc.) on a piece of paper. Discuss how these roles influence their self-perceptions--their identities. Which are most important in defining who they are? Which are least important? How has what they view as important for defining self been influenced by family, culture, peers? How would taking away one of those roles impact the importance of the other roles? How would it impact identity? Discuss situations in which people have roles removed (for instance, a woman who loses her husband and thus is no longer a "wife"; a man who loses his job and thus is no longer a "provider"; an athlete who becomes paralyzed and thus is no longer a "star"; etc.).

4. Have students take a typology test in class, such as the Myers-Briggs Type Indicator [Myers, I.B. (1962). <u>Manual: Myers-Briggs Type Indicator</u>. Palo Alto, CA: Consulting

Psychologists Press]. Discuss the types that emerge. Do the types match students' interests? Career ambitions? Weaknesses?

5. To illustrate Jung's concept of the **shadow** (the dark and unacceptable side of personality-- the unacceptable desires and motives that we would rather not admit), have students talk about the characters from films or novels that they personally find most scary or troubling.

6. To help students understand Horney's different coping styles, take a minute to artificially induce stress in your students (perhaps hand out a term-paper assignment that is exceptionally difficult and time-consuming and tell them that it is due two weeks from today; it is important that students believe you are serious). Then, either ask them to write down how they are feeling, or encourage them to express their feelings out loud (they may already be doing this). Tell them that this is not a real assignment, but that your purpose in handing it out was to allow them to see themselves "moving toward," "moving against," and "moving away" from the source of stress. See if they can agree as a group on at least one person who was visibly "moving away," one who was "moving against," and one who was "moving toward."

Recommended Outside Readings

Brome, V. (1981). Jung: Man and myth. New York: Atheneum Books.

Jung, C. (1961). Memories, dreams, reflections (Aniela Jaffe, Ed.). New York: Pantheon.

Bottome, P. (1957). Alfred Adler: A portrait from life. New York: Vanguard.

Quinn S. (1987). A mind of her own: The life of Karen Horney. New York: Simon & Schuster.

Horney, K. (1980). The adolescent diaries of Karen Horney. New York: Basic Books.

Coles, R. (1970). Erik Erikson: The growth of his work. Boston: Little Brown.

Erikson, E. (1963). Childhood and society. New York: W. W. Norton.

Erikson, E. (1993). Gandhi's truth: On the origins of militant nonviolence. NY: W. W. Norton.

Levinson, D. J., et al. (1978). The seasons of a man's life New York: Knopf.

Films / Videos

"The World Within." Covers quite a bit of Jungian theory, much of it in Jung's own words (has a portion of an actual interview with Jung). Gives a good sense of his personal life, as well as his line of philosophical thought. 60 minutes. 1990. Insight Media: 800-233-9910.

"Discussion with Dr. Carl Jung: Introversion-Extroversion and Other Contributions." Jung talks about his relationship with Freud and some of his own theories, including a discussion of archetypes. 36 minutes. 1968. PCR: Films and Video in the Behavioral Sciences.

"67,000 Dreams." Good focus on Jung's symbols and myths. 31 minutes, BBC Production. Films for the Humanities and Sciences: 800-257-5126.

"Erik Erikson: A Life's Work." Includes personal information about Erikson, as well as addressing his eight stages of development. 38 minutes. 1992. Insight Media: 800-233-9910.

CHAPTER 5: BIOLOGICAL ASPECTS

This chapter is unique in providing a comprehensive overview of biological influences on personality, but it is written in a way that is tied to other approaches and is easily understandable by students. For example, this chapter does not get into esoteric disputes from biology and genetics, but rather keeps the focus on personality. It can easily be integrated into courses that have not previously included a chapter on this topic.

Evolutionary effects and genetic abnormalities are of course important, but many biological influences are not genetic! For example, environmental toxins, physical disease, and biologically-based creations of environments and expectations are important biological influences on personality. This is too often ignored. This chapter challenges students to think for themselves about the role of biology, and re-evaluate common stereotypes. Importantly this chapter concludes with warnings about the political dangers of a simple-minded approach to biology and personality.

Possible Lecture Outline

I. Direct genetic effects
- A. Through process of natural selection certain adaptive or functional characteristics have been reinforced
  - 1. these characteristics include behavioral tendencies and emotions—"personality"
- B. Example of Angelman syndrome as a "personality" directly caused by genetic abnormality

II. Effects through temperament (activity, emotionality, sociability, aggression/impulsivity)
- A. Eysenck's theory links the introversion-extroversion dimension to the underlying nervous system
  - 1. posits introverts have a higher level of internal arousal and thus seek out less external stimulation (and vice versa)
- B. Zuckerman's theory posits that those high on "sensation seeking" are driven by a low level of internal arousal; sensation seekers are drawn to novel and exciting experiences
- C. Studies of twins reared in different environments have demonstrated impressive similarities between those with the same genetic make-up
  - 1. Still unclear how much of the similarity is genetically pre-programmed and how much is due to similarities in their separate environments, etc.
  - 2. Twin studies have helped to show that schizophrenia is genetically linked, but it's clear that it's not simply a genetic disease
    - a. structural abnormalities have been found in the brains of

schizophrenics
b. concordance between identical twins is far from perfect
3. Twin studies have also shown that homosexuality is linked to genetics
a. again genes don't tell the whole story
b. structural differences have also been found between the brains of homosexual as compared to heterosexual men
c. How might homosexuality be addressed from an evolutionary point of view? Perhaps through "kin selection" or some other yet-to-be-discovered process.

III. Effects through environmental toxins and physical illness
A. Toxins/drugs
1. "Mad as a hatter" derived from brain damage hatters suffered when exposed to mercury in hat-making factories
2. Lead poisoning and cognitive/behavioral deficits in children
3. Manganese miners and fighting behavior
4. Personality changes associated with illegal or prescription drugs
B. Disease
1. Van Gogh and the possibility of Meniere's disease
2. Personality changes as a result of Alzheimer's disease
3. Personality changes following stroke or CABG

IV. Effects from creation of environments
A. The process is cyclical, with certain temperamental characteristics predisposing us to certain experiences, which in turn mold our personalities
B. Physical characteristics may also influence the types of experiences we choose; may be related to underlying physiological characteristics
1. Sheldon's somatotypes (endomorphs, ectomorphs, and mesomorphs) provide an example of this type of thinking on a simple level

V. Effects from reactions of others
A. Physical characteristics (fat/thin; short/tall; beautiful/disfigured) influence the way others treat us and thereby mold our views of the world--our "personalities"

VI. Misuse of knowledge regarding genetics
A. Social Darwinism and the right to dominate/kill others
B. American immigration laws to limit "undesirables"
C. Eugenics and forced sterilization of various groups
D. Nazi dream of a "master race" and genocide
E. The Human Genome Project--what are the implications?

Classroom Activities, Discussion Topics, and Projects

1. Periodically, various news-magazine shows do stories on various types of discrimination. For instance, hidden cameras are used to show how blacks are treated differently than whites when shopping in department stores or trying to rent apartments, or to demonstrate how difficult it is for an overweight or unattractive person to get a job or a date when compared with a thinner, more attractive counterpart. Discuss how biological factors such as skin color, weight, and looks might affect personality through these environmental influences. How does this relate to environmental influences initiated by temperament?

2. Plastic surgery is becoming more and more common. We are well-aware of the outward, physical effects of such surgery, but what are some of the more subtle implications? Might people who have dramatic surgery eventually develop different "personalities"? What are the potentially positive outcomes? Are there any negative implications?

3. Compare and contrast Sheldon's and Eysenck's approaches to integrating biology and personality. What are the benefits of a more complex model? What are some of the factors that no model has yet been able to take into account?

4. Administer Zuckerman's Sensation Seeking Scale [Zuckerman, M., Eysenck, S., & Eysenck, H.J. (1978). Sensation seeking in England and America: Cross-cultural, age, and sex comparisons. Journal of Consulting and Clinical Psychology, 46, 139-149]. Discuss the overall score, as well as the subscale scores which may be derived. Identify the lowest and highest scorers in the class and interview them about their hobbies, likes, and dislikes (you may wish to have them leave the room and then call them in one at a time to be interviewed in front of the class). Have the rest of the class take notes on observed differences. Discuss implications for internal levels of arousal.

5. Multiple births are now common. If are any twins in the class (identical or fraternal), or friends of twins, use this to begin a discussion of biological influences on personality.

Recommended Outside Readings

Buss, A. H. & Plomin, R. (1984). Temperament: Early developing personality traits. Hillsdale, NJ: Erlbaum.

Buss, D. M. (1991). Evolutionary personality psychology. Annual Review of Psychology, 42, 459-492.

Eysenck, H.J. (1967). The biological basis of personality. Springfield, IL: Charles C. Thomas.

Zuckerman, M. (1979). Sensation seeking: Beyond the optimal level of arousal. Hillsdale, NJ: Erlbaum.

Ekman, P. (1973). Cross-cultural studies of facial expression. In P. Ekman (Ed.), Darwin and facial expression. New York: Academic Press.

Eibl-Eibesfeldt, I. (1972). Similarities and differences between cultures in expressive movements. In R. Hinde (Ed.), Non-verbal communication. Cambridge, MA: Cambridge University Press.

Films / Videos

"The Human Animal: Nature and Nurture." Looks at nature vs. nurture explanations for behavior. Uses twin studies and neurochemical correlates of particular behaviors to make the case that biology is important. Talks about how biological predispositions are influenced by the environment. Hosted by Phil Donahue. 52 minutes. 1986. Films for the Humanities and Sciences: 800-257-5126.

"What Makes Us Tick?" Looks at genetic and environmental influences of personality (makes a stronger case for genetics). 24 minutes. 1989. Films for the Humanities and Sciences: 800-257-5126.

"Face Value." Looks at Ekman's work on facial expression in New Guinea, as well as Melzoff's work on 2-week-old babies recognizing and imitating facial expressions. 38 minutes. 1990. Insight Media (800-233-9910) or Filmaker's Library.

"Awakenings." Story of Dr. Malcolm Sayer, a physician and researcher who finds a drug which will "awaken" the bodies and personalities of catatonic patients with a rare disease. 120 minutes. RCA/Columbia Pictures. 1990.

CHAPTER 6: BEHAVIORIST AND LEARNING ASPECTS

This chapter attempts to bring to life the power and controversy surrounding behaviorist and learning approaches to personality. Skinner's ideas, like those of Freud, Jung, Rogers, and the other giants of 20th century psychology, have profoundly affected how we think about ourselves and our society, and it is important for students to appreciate the intellectual origin of controversies over everything from token reward systems for schoolchildren and prisoners, to the role and operation of government.

As in other places in this book, this chapter does not shy away from pointing out competing views of utopia and of human free will. This chapter is best combined with the following chapter (on cognitive aspects) to achieve a broad understanding of the relevant issues of learning, thinking, social learning, and personality.

Possible Lecture Outline

I. Classical conditioning of personality
   A. Ivan Pavlov discovered the principle of classical conditioning
      1. unconditioned stimulus, conditioned stimulus, unconditioned response, conditioned response
      2. the principles of generalization, discrimination and extinction are also important
   B. These principles help us to explain emotional aspects of personality (that is, these responses can be conditioned)
   C. A complex dimension like neuroticism is more difficult to explain, but may be the result of the environmental requirement of discriminations that are too difficult
   D. Some organisms are more easily conditioned than others, and to different stimuli

II. Origins of a behaviorist approach
   A. Behaviorism was founded by Watson as a way of making personality psychology a testable science; his views were very deterministic
   B. Applied Pavlov's classical conditioning theory to "little Albert," an 11-month-old boy
      1. Watson believed most of personality was formed via classical conditioning, just as Albert's fear was formed
      2. Used systematic desensitization (repeated introduction of CS without pairing of UCS) to extinguish little Albert's fear

III. Radical behaviorism of B.F. Skinner
  A. Believed that environmental consequences control all types of behavior-- a radically deterministic view
    1. Developed the principle of "operant conditioning" in which behavior is changed by its consequences
      a. positive vs. negative reinforcement
      b. punishment vs. negative reinforcement
    2. Developed the "Skinner Box" (not his term) to mold behavior through operant conditioning
    3. Different reinforcement schedules have differing levels of success
      a. continuous vs. partial reinforcement
      b. ratio vs. interval schedules
      c. fixed vs. variable schedules
    4. Skinner's novel Walden Two describes a utopian community in which behavior is controlled via operant conditioning techniques; his later non-fiction book, Beyond Freedom and Dignity, formalized these ideas
  B. An example of current research based on Skinnerian principles is that in which Type A behavior pattern was reduced in a group of Japanese men using operant conditioning methods
  C. Skinner believed biological factors determined an organism's ability to learn behaviors in response to reinforcement
  D. Skinner acknowledged human emotions, but believed them to irrelevant to behavior

IV. Other learning approaches to personality: the desire to combine behaviorism with an understanding of the internal characteristics of the organism
  A. Role of internal drives: Clark Hull
    1. Hull was particularly interested in "habits" which he saw as simple associations between stimulus and response
    2. Saw that responses that lead to goal acquisition could themselves be reinforcing
    3. Paid attention to the internal state of the organism while emphasizing the role of environmental reinforcers
  B. Social Learning Theory (SLT): Dollard and Miller
    1. SLT posits that our habits are built up in terms of a hierarchy of acquired secondary drives-- this is termed a "habit hierarchy"
    2. The idea of secondary drives explains personality constructs (they are learned secondary drives)
      a. the idea of secondary drives in relation to attachment was examined by Harlow
    3. Dollard and Miller agreed that Freud had isolated critical periods of child development, but their explanations involved the learning that occurred during those periods

4. How can mental illness be explained?
    a. approach-avoidance conflict (being drawn both to and away from something)
    b. approach-approach conflict (being drawn simultaneously to two equally attractive choices)
    c. avoidance-avoidance conflict (being confronted with two equally unattractive choices)
5. Frustration-aggression hypothesis: argues that aggression always results when an organism's progress toward a goal is blocked

V. Evaluation
  A. Behaviorism has forced the field of personality to be much more rigorous and scientifically sound
  B. Radical behaviorism has been limited by its refusal to take internal mental structures and functions into account
  C. Behaviorists as a whole are unconcerned with phenomena that aren't quantifiable; if it doesn't fit into an experimental design it's often ignored

Classroom Activities, Discussion Topics, and Projects

1. Discuss different types of reinforcement schedules (continuous vs. partial or intermittent; ratio vs. interval). What are the advantages of each? If we want to create a behavior that is resistant to extinction, which schedule of reinforcement would be best? Why?

2. Take two minutes and write down the situations in your life in which you are reinforced. Share these with the class, and discuss whether each represents a continuous or partial schedule, and a ratio or interval schedule. What are the strongest reinforcers on your list? What reinforcements are weak? Are there negative reinforcements?

3. Draw and briefly describe a Skinner box (or bring in a real box). Discuss how Skinner used this box for both animals and children. What are the ethical implications; would this be approved by an IRB committee in this decade? How are our environments like big Skinner boxes?

4. Discuss specialized societies (some cults, religious groups, etc.) that try to approximate many of the ideals voiced in Skinner's Walden Two and Beyond Freedom and Dignity. Where does the idea of brainwashing fit into the picture? How have these societies turned out? What are the pros and cons of creating such a society? Does anyone really have "free will"? Is freedom important enough to sacrifice for? What are we willing to sacrifice?

5. Define each of the following in terms of how the conditioning principles discussed in class might apply to the real world: Hours of deprivation, Skinner box, reinforcement, pellet dispenser, secondary reinforcer, discriminative stimuli, and reinforcement schedules. For example, hours of deprivation for a rat in a Skinner box might be equivalent to our desires or aversions; the Skinner box itself might be equivalent to some of the situations in which we find ourselves; and the pellet dispenser might represent people or social institutions which have control over rewards.

6. Have students identify one habit or behavior in themselves that they would like to change, along with a simple structure of rewards and punishments which they will use to operantly condition themselves. For example, a student may wish to eliminate his/her habit of snacking between meals and may decide to "punish" him/herself with 10 pushups every time snacking occurs and reward him/herself with a dollar each at each meal when snacking prior to the meal has not occurred. Have students keep a diary of their behaviors for two weeks (a diary in chart form works nicely for illustrative purposes). At the end of two weeks discuss the observed patterns of behavior in class.

7. Assign small groups of students to do research on an assigned cult, paying special attention to the "brainwashing" techniques the cult uses. Have them identify ways of "deprogramming" cult members. Discuss whether "deprogramming" is also "brainwashing" – what is the difference between conforming to societal norms and being controlled by society? What does this tell us about the social creation of personality? Is personality simply "learned" as a radical behaviorist would have us believe?

8. Arrange a debate between students who think that it makes sense to analyze and shape humans through reward and punishment schedules and those who think that there are serious problems with such an approach. Try to keep the arguments focused on testable issues (rather than vague assertions).

Recommended Outside Readings

Pavlov, I. P. (1927). Conditioned reflexes. Oxford, England: Oxford University Press.

Skinner, B. F. (1974). About behaviorism. New York: Knopf.

Skinner, B. F. (1971). Beyond freedom and dignity. New York: Knopf.

Skinner, B.F. (1938). The behavior of organisms. New York: Appleton-Century-Crofts.

Skinner, B.F. (1948). Walden two. New York: Macmillan.

Skinner, B. F., & Vaughan, M. E. (1983). Enjoy old age: A program of self-management. New York: W. W. Norton.

Bjork, D. W. (1993). B. F. Skinner: A life. New York: Basic Books.

Films / Videos

"Discovering Psychology: Learning." Describes the principles of classical and operant conditioning (Pavlov, Thorndike, Skinner). It is part 8 in a series. 30 minutes. Annenberg/CPB Multimedia Collection: 800-532-7637. 1990.

"Learning." Also looks at classical and operant conditioning, but includes an interview with Skinner, and has an example of a child who is hyperactive and is helped with operant conditioning. 30 minutes. 1990. Insight Media: 800-233-9910.

"Conversation with B.F. Skinner." An interview with Skinner in which he talks about the need for a behaviorist-designed culture. Touches on important concepts in Skinnerian theory. 20 minutes. 1972. CRM Films: 760-431-9800.

"Token Economy: Behaviorism Applied." Looks at the use of tokens in environments structured to provide systematic reinforcement of desired behaviors. Includes a demonstration with children at a mental health facility in Illinois. 20 minutes. 1972. CRM Films: 760-431-9800.

CHAPTER 7: COGNITIVE ASPECTS

This straightforward chapter applies basic cognitive notions to personality, and thus includes field theory, field dependence, schemas, constructs, scripts, and attributions. The main classic theorist is George Kelly, and the modern counterparts are attributional models of helplessless (e.g. Seligman). Bandura's social-cognitive learning theory is presented in detail as a sophisticated modern theory that integrates many key cognitive and behavioral notions, and significant attention is also given to Julian Rotter's notions of locus of control and social learning. Although some texts include some of these matters in a behaviorist/learning chapter, we find that many students understand this material better *after* they understand the work of Pavlov, Skinner, and Dollard and Miller.

This chapter also gets students thinking about how computers seem to have personalities.

Possible Lecture Outline

I. Perception and cognition as the core of personality
  A. Roots in Gestalt psychology
    1. We seek meaning in our environments
    2. We organize sensations into meaningful perceptions
    3. Complex stimuli are not reducible to the sum of their parts
  B. Lewin's field theory
    1. Life space
    2. Focus on issues related to separateness of different areas of the life space
    3. Contemporaneous causation
    4. Field dependent people are easily influenced by the context or "field" they are functioning in
      a. rod-and-frame task
  C. Field dependence as a personality variable
    1. First explored as a personality variable by Witkin and Asch
    2. Some of the demonstrated associations with field dependence are
      a. children's play preferences
      b. socialization patterns
      c. career choices
      d. preferred interpersonal distance during conversation
      e. level of eye contact
    3. Small, consistent gender differences (women more field dependent)
    4. Field dependence also shown to vary cross-culturally

D. Schema theory
    1. Piaget proposed that children understand the world through cognitive structures called "schemas" which build upon one another as the child develops (adults have schemas, too)
    2. Schemas play an important role in determining how we think and act
        a. "script" is a schema for a familiar ritual

E. Categorization: organizing our experiences by grouping into categories
    1. Ability to screen out unimportant/irrelevant stimuli
    2. Ability to glean rich information from fleeting facial expressions
    3. The step from useful category to dangerous stereotype is small
        a. confirmation bias is seen in the use of stereotypes

F. Control of attention is an important factor which allows us to function efficiently
    1. We notice salient environmental features and combine these with our current goals to decide where to direct our attention
    2. Individual differences in attention: to what degree is attention under conscious control (e.g. Attention Deficit Disorder [ADD])?

II. Humans as scientists

A. Kelly's Personal Construct Theory posits that people are like scientists, actively trying to discover the world around them (a constructivist view)

B. Behavior is guided by interpretations of events and expectations of future events

C. Kelly believed each person's system of constructs is different and thus each person has a unique personality "theory"
    1. Role Construct Repertory Test (Rep Test) assesses an individual's personal construct system

III. Social intelligence: people differ in interpersonal skills, just like they differ on all sorts of other dimensions

A. There is a cluster of abilities that is important for successfully relating to others

B. A similar idea is proposed by Gardner's "multiple intelligences" theory

IV. Explanatory style as a personality variable

A. Explanatory style: characteristic way of interpreting life-events (e.g. optimism vs. pessimism)
    1. An optimistic explanatory style is generally more adaptive, although excessive or inappropriate optimism isn't healthy
    2. People with an optimistic explanatory style usually deal with stress more successfully (often take an information-seeking and situation/self-monitoring approach)

B. The cognitive consequence is that those who cope by blunting or repressing information (typical of the pessimistic explanatory style) will later have less cognitive information available to them

V. Bandura's social-cognitive learning theory
   A. Self-system: set of cognitive processes a person uses to perceive, evaluate, and regulate his/her own behavior so it's functionally efficient and appropriate
   B. Observational learning (also called vicarious learning or modeling): learning a behavior by watching another rather than performing it oneself (illustrated with Bobo Doll studies)
   C. May or may not perform learned behavior
      1. Outcome expectancies important in determining performance of learned behavior
      2. Complexity of the behavior, attributes of the model, and attributes of the observer also play a role in determining whether or not a learned behavior is performed
   D. Observational learning explains how we can learn to inhibit unacceptable behavior without first performing it
   E. Observational learning requires four components
      1. Attention
      2. Retention
      3. Motor reproduction
      4. Motivation
   F. Self-regulation (goals, planning, self-reinforcement, and self-punishment)
   G. Self-efficacy: expectancy about one's own ability to be successful (determines whether we try to act at all, how long we persist in difficult times, and how successes and failures affect future behavior; based on four kinds of information
      1. Personal performance experiences
      2. Vicarious experiences
      3. Verbal persuasion
      4. Emotional reactions

VI. Rotter's social learning and locus of control approaches
   A. Behavior depends upon outcome expectancy and reinforcement value
   B. Behavior potential: likelihood that a behavior will be performed in a particular situation
      1. Generalized expectancies carry more weight in novel situations
      2. Specific expectancies are used in familiar situations
   C. Rotter's six psychological needs which stem from biological needs (these are satisfied by secondary reinforcers)
      1. Recognition-status
      2. Dominance
      3. Independence
      4. Protection-dependency
      5. Love and affection
      6. Physical comfort

D. "Psychological situation" represents an individual's unique set of potential behaviors, outcome expectancies, and reinforcement potential
E. Locus of control (internal vs. external): beliefs about one's ability to affect outcomes
    1. More recently, there seem to be three semi-orthogonal dimensions
        a. luck
        b. powerful others
        c. internality

VII. Attributional model of learned helplessness
    A. Seligman describes learned helplessness as a situation in which one learns that negative events can't be avoided
        1. belief learned through repeated, uncontrollable exposure to negative event;
        2. belief persists even when negative event *is* later avoidable

VIII. Humans as computers: artificial intelligence
    A. Is simulating cognitive tasks the same thing as creating a "personality"? No.
        1. Personality-like characteristics can be programmed
        2. We may tend to make "personality" attributions even when no "personality" exists
            a. the Turing test

Classroom Activities, Discussion Topics, and Projects

1. How does our innate tendency to categorize things interact with our tendency to stereotype? Are stereotypes ever good? What functions can stereotypes serve? Why is it that stereotypes are so often self-perpetuating? Can stereotypes create self-fulfilling prophecies?

2. How do we diagnose attention deficit disorder (ADD) and attention deficit hyperactivity disorder (ADHD)? Are these disorders over-diagnosed? Can these problems be "fixed" or are they stable, trait-like characteristics? What are the pros and cons of treating ADD and ADHD with drugs?

3. Have students take a shortened version of Kelly's Role Rep test, and discuss the findings.

4. Have students take an Embedded Figures Test. Discuss situations in which being field-dependent would be advantageous, and situations in which it would be preferable to be field-independent. Have students integrate the information on conditioning from chapter 6 with the idea of field-independence/dependence—that is, what kind of person might be expected to have a more malleable personality (if, in fact, "personality" is behavior)?

5. Have students write out a detailed "script" for a first date. Compare within the class to see how closely these scripts match. Discuss how the schemas and scripts we have influence our perception of the world and influence who we are.

Recommended Outside Readings

Bandura, A. (1977). Social learning theory. Englewood Cliffs, NJ: Prentice-Hall.

Bandura, A. (1997). Self-efficacy: The exercise of control. New York: W. H. Freeman.

Kelly, G. A. (1969). Clinical psychology and personality: The selected papers of George Kelly. Edited by Brendan Maher. New York: Wiley.

Mischel, W. (1973). Toward a cognitive social learning reconceptualization of personality. Psychological Review, 80, 252-283.

Rotter, J. B. (1966). Generalized expectancies for internal vs. external control of reinforcement. Psychological Monographs, 80, (No. 609).

Hastorf, A. H., & Cantril, H. (1954). They saw a game: A case study. Journal of Abnormal and Social Psychology, 49, 129-134.

Seligman, M. E. P. (1991). Learned optimism. New York: A. A. Knopf.

Films / Videos

"Dr. Jean Piaget with Dr. Barbel Inhelder: Part I." Goes through each of the cognitive stages of development. Looks at motivation, learning, and perception. (Part II has Piaget talking about Freud's work and Jensen's work on intelligence in blacks; also reaction to misuse of his theories.) 40 minutes (Part I). PCR: Films and Video in the Behavioral Sciences. [Insight Media also has something called "Jean Piaget" that looks nearly identical-- also a 2-part series.] 1969.

"Albert Bandura." Bandura himself describes his approach to the study of personality, and compares it to other approaches. Part I includes discussion of how he developed his theories, behavior modification, social learning. Part II covers the Bobo doll research, morality, and violence in the media. 28 minutes (Part I) and 29 minutes (Part II). 1988. Insight Media: 800-233-9910.

"The Diagnosis and Treatment of Attention Deficit Disorder in Children." Looks at the behavior of children with ADHD at home, in regular schools, and in a specialized alternative school for children with the disorder. Discusses drug and behavioral treatments. Includes commentary by psychiatrists Ratey and Hallowell, who are prominent in this field. 27 minutes. 1995. Films for the Humanities and Sciences: 800-257-3767.

CHAPTER 8 : TRAIT AND SKILL ASPECTS

Chapter 8 provides a comprehensive overview of trait approaches to personality, from the early work of Allport and Cattell through significant discussion of the modern "Big Five" dimensions. Motives and skills are also given significant attention. Since this is an area of both important past theory and active current research, special care is taken to organize material carefully while much ground is covered.

Students are generally somewhat familiar with trait approaches and are fascinated to learn how to be more scientific and analytic in their understandings of themselves and others. Many of these issues are taken up again in Chapter 10, when we discuss person-situation interaction aspects of personality.

Possible Lecture Outline

I. Early history of trait approaches
   - A. Hippocrates described four bodily "humors" (sanguine, melancholic, choleric, phlegmatic) to explain temperament
   - B. Theophrastus created "character sketches" which we still recognize today
   - C. Forward-thinking individuals like Darwin, Galton, and Freud, along with the development of statistical techniques, set the stage for modern trait-theory

II. Beginnings of the modern trait approach
   - A. Jung's use of the terms "introversion" and "extraversion" and his concepts of "sensing-intuiting" and "thinking-feeling" set in motion the modern study of personality traits
   - B. Allport identified thousands of personality adjectives in the English language as a means of understanding personality
     1. Was very aware of human complexity (and no fan of the behaviorists or Cattell)
     2. Allport simplified or defined personality in terms of functional equivalence; traits which groups of individuals shared he called "common traits"
     3. Allport argued the importance of an idiographic approach to personality; he looked at people's "personal dispositions"; the most powerful of these he termed "cardinal dispositions"
   - C. Cattell used factor analysis to derive "traits" from Allport's list of personality adjectives; based on his analyses he argued that there are 16 basic personality traits
     1. Cattell coined the terms Q-data (questionnaire data), T-data (test data), and L-data (life data) to describe the various types of information one should have to adequately measure personality

III. The Big Five
  A. Over the past four decades a vast body of research has converged on the idea that five dimensions are adequate for describing personality in a broad, general sense.
    1. The "Big 5" are generally termed: Extraversion, Agreeableness, Openness, Neuroticism, and Conscientiousness
    2. As yet, there is no biologically-based evidence that these five constructs are "real"
      a. perhaps the agreement re: five broad traits is due to the implicit personality theories of the raters (that is, what we "see" and "don't see" may be biased in ways we don't recognize)
    3. Note that the Big 5 are general categories-- even Big 5 proponents recognize that they are not sufficient to fully explain personality (for example, six facets make up each Big 5 dimension)
  B. Not all theorists think 5 is the correct number of dimensions
    1. Cattell continues to assert that there are 16 basic personality dimensions
    2. Eysenck believed that all characteristics derive from only three basic traits (which are based on biological systems): extraversion, neuroticism, and psychoticism

IV. Other ways of looking at personality
  A. Types: the idea that there are discrete categories of people
  B. Motives: internal psycho-biological forces that help induce particular behavior patterns
    1. Murray describes these motives as "needs " (nAch, nPower, nAff, etc.)
    2. Cantor describes these motives as "life tasks"
    3. Emmons calls them "personal strivings"
  C. Expressive style: individual patterns in gesturing, body incline, voice cues, etc.
    1. expressiveness (the ease with which people's emotions are "read" from behavior" involves intensity, expansiveness, animation, and dynamism in both verbal and nonverbal behaviors
    2. expressive style is related to various personality traits, including extraversion and dominance
  D. Skills: abilities which differ from person to person
    1. intelligence is a much-studied ability; some theories argues that there are various types of intelligence
    2. "social intelligence" or "emotional intelligence" combine ideas of non-traditional intelligence with ideas of nonverbal social skills

Classroom Activities, Discussion Topics, and Projects

1. Have students work in pairs to rate various popular figures (sports stars, movie actors, etc.) on each of the Big 5 dimensions. See how well pairs of students agree. Discuss what information was used to make the ratings. Discuss whether it might have been helpful to have more categories (for instance, 16), or whether they could have narrowed it to three broad categories.

2. Discuss the trait of "openness" or "intellect." What does it really capture? Why has it been more difficult than the others to define?

3. Have students graphically profile someone high vs. low on each of the Big 5 dimensions as follows: A) Divide the class into five groups and assign each group a trait. B) Each group will be given two large pieces of butcher paper and a felt-tipped pen. C) Instruct the groups to use one of the sheets of paper for someone high and the other for someone low on their trait; they should write this identification at the top of the paper. D) Have the groups work together to create six "quotations" or statements on each piece of paper; each statement should embody as completely as possible one of the facets of that trait. For example, on the "high Conscientiousness" sheet one might find comments such as: "I am very good at my job" (competence) and "It's important to me to have a clean house" (order). E) When students have completed their work have the groups present their illustrations to the class. Alternatively, this may be presented as a quiz-game to the class (let the class identify what the broad trait is, and name each of the facets themselves).

4. Trait psychology has been greatly influenced by the area of IQ testing (and vice versa). Discuss Gardner's multiple intelligences. How might the field of personality psychology (especially trait psychology) have been different if we had started out with the idea of multiple intelligences?

5. Have students try to map Cattell's 16 personality factors and Eysenck's 3 personality traits onto the Big Five dimensions. Discuss areas where the fit is good and areas that don't correspond as well.

6. Have some students engage in some behaviors that reveal something about their expressive style (e.g. dance, jump, lecture, write) in front of the class, and have the other students try to infer something about personality. Discuss issues of reliability and validity.

Recommended Outside Readings

Loevinger, J. (1987). Paradigms of personality (pp. 93-120; The psychometric approach: Traits). New York: W.H. Freeman.

McCrae, R. R., & Costa, P. T., Jr. (1990). Personality in adulthood. New York: Guilford Press.

Guilford, J. P. (1959). Personality. New York: McGraw-Hill.

Mischel, W. (1968). Personality and assessment. New York: Wiley.

Allport, G. W. (1966). Traits revisited. American Psychologist, 21, 1-10.

Jung, C. G. (1924). Psychological types. New York: Harcourt Brace.

Eysenck, H. J., & Rachman, S. (1965). The causes and cures of neurosis. San Diego, CA: Robert R. Knapp.

John, O. P. (1990). The "Big Five" factor taxonomy: Dimensions of personality in the natural language and in questionnaires. In L. A. Pervin (Ed.), Handbook of personality: Theory and research. New York: Guilford.

Films / Videos

"Giftedness: With Ups and Downs." Looks at two gifted children who were frustrated in school and even thought to have disorders due to their misbehavior. Discusses the inability of many schools to deal with unusually bright or gifted children. (Subtitles.) 28 minutes. 1990. Filmakers Library: 212-808-4980.

"Pain of Shyness." Phillip Zimbardo discusses techniques which help some people to overcome shyness, a "trait" which many people share and which, when severe, can be quite handicapping. 17 minutes. 1987. Filmakers Library: 212-808-4980.

"Hans Eysenck." A presentation by Eysenck himself of his theory of personality types. Includes a description of factor analysis as a methodology. 32 minutes. 1970. Insight Media: 800-233-9910.

CHAPTER 9: HUMANISTIC AND EXISTENTIAL ASPECTS

Students often find this topic appealing, repulsive, and/or confusing, and so significant effort was made to bring alive key humanistic and existential theories and concepts. This chapter explains the origins of this perspective, and points out why it sometimes provokes so much passion.

Most students will relate to Maslow's concepts of a need hierarchy and of self-actualization, so these are good places to turn if the other theorists initially leave them with blank looks. Also, many current-day results of the "human potential movement" are good points to provoke discussion and interest.

Possible Lecture Outline

I. Existentialism, in simple terms, is an area of philosophy concerned with the meaning of human existence
  A. It is non-positivist in nature (positivists focus on laws governing reality; non-positivists focus on the subjectivity of "reality"), and as such, it is non-deterministic
  B. Focus on "being-in-the-world"
  C. Much of it is phenomenological in nature
    1. subjective realities are considered to be valid data for study

II. Humanism is a philosophical approach which emphasizes human worth and values (sometimes called the "third force," with psychoanalysis and behaviorism being the other two)
  A. Emphasizes human activity, awareness, and power to change self
  B. Draws from existentialism the idea that our existence is dependent on our reactions to others
  C. Foundation of the "human potential movement"

III. Important elements in existential/humanistic psychology
  A. Love
    1. Fromm argued that love requires knowledge, effort, and experience (contrary to popular belief that is just "happens")
    2. Love allows us to overcome alienation while maintaining personal integrity
    3. Fromm incorporates many fundamental ideas drawn from religion and mysticism into his understanding of personality
  B. Responsibility
    1. Rogers believed that people have an inherent tendency toward

growth and maturation, but they are personally responsible for achieving them
2. According to Rogers, the important issues to be dealt with are defined by the individual; Rogerian therapy is non-directive and incorporates "unconditional positive regard"

C. Anxiety and dread
1. Rollo May sees anxiety as triggered by a threat to core values of existence; much of his work has focused on isolation, anxiety, and the individual's search for meaning in life
2. One example of the impact of this type of thinking is the popularity of "support groups" for people dealing with various illnesses and other anxiety-provoking experiences

D. Self-actualization
1. The innate process by which one grows spiritually and realizes one's ultimate potential
2. Although many psychologists have talked about self-actualization (Jung and James were first), it's most closely associated with Maslow
3. Maslow proposed a hierarchy of needs, whereby we must first ensure our survival, then pursue higher aims such as finding security, love, self-esteem, etc.
4. Self-actualization (the top of Maslow's hierarchy) is characterized by "peak experiences" (experiences where we become completely absorbed by the event or the activity; time seems to "stand still")
5. The "Personal Orientation Inventory" is one scale that attempts to assess self-actualization; it seems to capture at least some aspects of a healthy personality

Classroom Activities, Discussion Topics and Projects

1. Assign several students to different "problems" and assign several more students to the position of "Rogerian Therapist." Have the students role-play the therapeutic encounter, while the rest of the class takes notes on the interaction. Discuss what occurs.

2. Discuss how the ideas of philosophers like Kirkegaard and Nietzsche have influenced the humanistic movement.

3. Have students think of the last time they were completely engaged (in an enjoyable way) in an activity. Discuss the aspects of these experiences. Do they conform to the criteria of "peak experiences"? Then have students think back over their their most enjoyable memories. Are most of these memories of "peak experiences"?

4. Have students identify themselves on Maslow's hierarchy of needs. Discuss what they are doing to achieve the needs of their particular levels and move to the next level.

5. Have students make a list of people who they believe are self-actualized. (Presumably this will be a more modern list than that of Maslow.) What qualities of these individuals do they admire? Are there any negative characteristics?

Recommended Outside Readings

Lowrey, R. (1973). A. H. Maslow: An intellectual portrait. Monterey, CA: Brooks-Cole.

Maslow, A. H. (1970). Motivation and personality. New York: Harper & Row.

Maslow, A. H. (1971). The farther reaches of human nature. New York: Viking Press.

Rogers, C. (1951). Client-centered therapy: Its current practice, implications, and theory. Boston, MA: Houghton Mifflin.

Rogers, C., & Stevens, B. (1967). Person to person: The problem of being human. New York: Simon & Schuster.

Wexler, D. A., & Rice, L. N. (1974). Innovations in client-centered therapy. New York: Wiley.

Csikszentmihalyi, M., & Larson, R. (1984). Being adolescent: Conflict and growth in the teenage years. New York: Basic Books.

Frankl, V. E. (1984). Man's search for meaning. (Revised and updated.) New York: Washington Square Press.

Films / Videos

"The Human Dilemma: Rollo May." Discusses his theory of the human condition. Talks about how happiness results from an appreciation of the hard things in life. 90 minutes. 1988. Insight Media: 800-233-9910.

"Carl Rogers." A 2-part series that compares the humanistic model with other theories of personality. Part 1 looks at motivation, perception, learning, and client-centered therapy. Part 2 has Rogers discussing his views on education and unrest in the 1960s. Each part is 50 minutes. 1969. Insight Media: 800-233-9910.

"Being Abraham Maslow." Maslow discusses his childhood and school years, talking about his early aspirations, his strengths, and his weaknesses; then moves on to his adulthood, marriage and fatherhood, and looks toward the end of life. Addresses his views on Freud and behaviorism. 30 minutes. 1972. PCR: Films and Videos in the Behavioral Sciences.

CHAPTER 10: PERSON-SITUATION INTERACTIONIST ASPECTS

This unique chapter reveals the realization of many older notions in combination with the most modern theories and research. If personality is stable, why do behaviors vary so much? By using Lewin, Murray, and Sullivan to lay the groundwork, the influential ideas of the interactionists are made more sensible and understandable to students. Also, by this point in the course, students should be ready to think in a critical and sophisticated manner about personality.

Person -situation interactionist approaches endeavor to take into account the many ways personality "is realized in" or "unfolds in" or "interacts with" the situational context. Although many of the most modern notions about personality are presented in this chapter, it is important to recognize that they derive from and are closely tied to the other seven basic aspects of personality considered in the book. This chapter is also a good place for the instructor to introduce his or her own favorite modern theories or notions about personality.

Possible Lecture Outline

I. Few people are totally honest or dishonest; then what is personality? How does it affect behavior?
  - A. Lewin's equation: B = f (P, E) [behavior is a function of personality and environment]
  - B. Allport believed we have consistent patterns in predispositions, but behavior is manifest uniquely in each situation
  - C. Murray posited internal "needs" and external "press" which worked in concert

II. Henry Stack Sullivan
  - A. Importance of "chums" and adolescent psychosocial threats of loneliness, isolation, rejection;
    1. Psychological health determined to large degree by reactions of others
  - B. We experience similar social situations over and over
    1. Drew on G. H. Mead's ideas of the "social self" and Sapir's views of the importance of culture
  - C. We become different "people" in different situations; the situation elicits the personality (note the "illusion of individuality" which describes belief in just one "personality")

III. Motivation and goals: Henry Murray
    A. Murray is considered a primary founder of the interactionist approach to personality;
    B. Combined ideas of unconscious motivations with those of environmental pressures and traits
    C. Because he focused on the richness of life and saw "personality" as a dynamic process, he called his theory a "personological system"
        1. Internal needs and motivations
        2. Environmental press
    D. Typical combinations of needs and presses termed "thema"
        1. Measured with the Thematic Apperception Test (TAT)
    E. The work of McAdams provides a modern example of Murray's influence
        1. Studies the "whole person" through biographies

IV. Other influences on Murray's approach
    A. Lewin's contemporaneous causation (behavior is caused *at that moment* as a function of a variety of influences
    B. Ideas of behaviorists, such as Skinner, were adapted by Murray as he incorporated situational influences into his theory
    C. Humanistic notions of internal motivations toward creativity and self-fulfillment

V. Modern interactionist approaches: Walter Mischel
    A. Mischel's 1968 argument that behavior varies so much by situation that the concept of personality traits makes little sense
        1. Correlations of behavior with personality or of behavior across situations are generally .30 or less
            a. assumes a simple model of the personality-behavior relationship
            b. assumes that a correlation of .30 is "small"
    B. More recently, Mischel has looked at individual differences in meanings people give to stimuli and reinforcements (called "strategies")
        1. Competencies: abilities and knowledge
        2. Encoding strategies: schemas and mechanisms used to encode information
        3. Expectancies: what we expect to happen in response to our efforts/behaviors
        4. Plans

VI. Other modern developments from interactionist perspective
   A. Implicit personality theory
      1. Observers tend to make attributions to personality; actors are more likely to make situational attributions
      2. Stereotypes help simplify the world
      3. People tend to overestimate the consistency of their own behaviors
   B. The power of situations: sometimes they are so powerful that they override personality effects (e.g. reactions to a fire in a crowded theater)
   C. Consistency within situations: problem of how to classify situations-- where would we *expect* behavioral consistency?
   D. Consistency averaged across situations
      1. Reliability issues (is one sample behavior a reliable indicator of personality?)
      2. Appropriateness of situation for being associated with particular trait
      3. Averaging cross-situational behaviors helps to deal with both of these issues
   E. Personal vs. social situations; personal vs. social selves
      1. Field independence: characteristic which enables one to judge an object, disregarding background influences (in social situations, such person may act more independently)
      2. Field dependence: characteristic which forces one to rely on background influences to make judgments (in social situations, such person may conform to situational demands)
      3. Low self-monitoring (less sensitive to reactions and expectations of others, so may show more consistent behavior across situations) vs.
         High self-monitoring (more sensitive to social influence that varies across situations, thus more difficult to see personality)
      4. Social identity vs. personal identity
   F. Seeking and creating situations
      1. We seek situations that reinforce self-conceptions, making for more "personality consistency"
      2. Consistency also results in part from our conscious efforts
   G. Time: Longitudinal data necessary to understand how personality develops over time
      1. Block and Block's longitudinal study at Berkeley
      2. Caspi's study of the "life course" and the individual's creation of the life course through choosing environments in which to live and through interpreting situations
      3. Terman's Life-Cycle Study

H. Readiness
   1. Each experience has its effects in the context of previous experience
   2. We are more affected by certain environments at certain times of our lives
   3. Both of these concepts come into play in Lorenz's ideas of "critical periods" and "imprinting"
      a. Lorenz's ideas focused on critical developmental periods, but we may also imagine more transient "critical periods" or times of "readiness" (based on circadian rhythms, etc.)

Classroom Activities, Discussion Topics, and Projects

1. Have each person in the class describe a recent situation in which they made a personality attribution about someone they didn't know, based on his/her behavior. Have classmates come up with alternative explanations for the behavior.

2. Give the class a brief scenario, such as "you are at the beach alone, planning to read and relax, when suddenly you see a group of friends." Have class members write down what they would do. Then, have them discuss the reasons they made those choices-- those behaviors. How might an outside observer interpret their behavior?

3. Have students identify strong situations—situations in which they believe the personality of the individual has little chance to shine through. Next have them identify weak situations—situations in which the person has a lot of behavioral latitude. Discuss whether or not we take the strength of the situation into account as we should when evaluating the behavior of others.

4. Discuss the ways in which personality may affect the environments we choose, and how these environments may in turn strengthen the personality characteristics that lead us to choose the environment in the first place. To what degree is it possible to change personality by changing environments?

Recommended Outside Readings

McAdams, D. P. (1988). Biography, narrative, and lives: An introduction. Journal of Personality, 56, 1-18.

Mischel, W. (1977). On the future of personality assessment. American Psychologist, 32, 246-254.

Mischel, W. (1990). Personality dispositions revisited and revised: A view after three decades. In L. A. Pervin (Ed.), Handbook of personality: Theory and research. New York: Guilford.

Funder, D. C. (1983). The "consistency" controversy and the accuracy of personality judgments. Journal of Personality, 48, 473-493.

Funder, D. C., & Ozer, D. J. (1983). Behavior as a function of the situation. Journal of Personality and Social Psychology, 44, 107-112.

Films / Videos

"Discovering Psychology: The Power of the Situation." Looks at how situational forces can change beliefs and behavior; examines the social psychological point of view, but doesn't say much about personality. 1990. Annenberg/CPB Multimedia Collection: 800-532-7637.

"Little Girl Lost: A Troubled Adolescent." The story of a young girl's (Joanne Shaver) life and early death at the age of 17. She came from a seemingly average family but became involved in a life of drugs, running away, and prostitution. Provides a good basis for discussion of the role of environment vs. person in determining behavior. 1993. Filmmaker's Library: 212-808-4980.

CHAPTER 11: MALE-FEMALE DIFFERENCES

This chapter begins the section on "applications to individual differences," which shows how the theory and research of the eight basic perspectives can be applied to fascinating and important issues in science and society. In particular, chapter 11, which focuses on male-female differences, reveals how characteristics that are obviously heavily influenced by biology cannot be fully understood without also taking into account social, developmental, and cultural influences on personality. Any of the four chapters in this section may be skipped or taken out of sequence, but students are likely to find them the most appealing and "relevant."

Are there gender-based psychological differences? What is the etiology (causal origin) of these differences? How do different personality theories explain how these differences emerge and how they are maintained? It is a rare college student who is not fascinated by such questions.

Possible Lecture Outline

I. Do males and females differ?
  A. Physical and physiological differences
  B. Studies have shown that subjects can agree on many personality characteristics that are "masculine" or "feminine"
    1. Studies of validity and effect size show that there's substantial overlap in male and female characteristics
  C. Reliable gender differences in psychological areas:
    1. Spatial abilities
    2. Verbal abilities
    3. Communication
    4. Aggression
  D. A brief history of gender differences in personality
    1. 4,000 to 6,000 years ago females portrayed as nurturing, fertility-objects, passive; men portrayed as hunters, aggressive, active
    2. Women seen as less worthy, less valuable than men
      a. Plato: women as weak, inferior
      b. Aristotle: women as incomplete, incompetent
      c. Biblically, men were in power, had higher moral authority
    3. Women evolutionarily designed to give birth, nurture, therefore this should be their primary role

4. Freud posited that psychological reactions to genital differences yielded gender differences
5. Current theories postulate an interaction of biological and environmental factors to produce "masculine" and "feminine" traits

II. Biological influences on gender differences
- A. Chromosomes: XX vs. XY
    1. Testes develop in XY embryos; produce androgen
    2. Androgen (or lack thereof) initiates development of male vs. female genitalia
- B. Androgen exposure may also affect brain development and personality
    1. Evidence from animal studies
    2. Evidence from studies of humans with prenatal genetic or hormonal anomalies (e.g. XXX, XXY, XYY; Turner's [XO] syndrome)

III. Later changes in hormones and physical development
- A. Major differences in proportions of hormones produced by males vs. females starting at puberty
- B. Cyclic vs. non-cyclic nature of hormonal fluctuation
    1. Emotionality and mood swings, etc.
    2. Hysteria and the "wandering" uterus
    3. Social and political implications

IV. Brain differences related to gender are still largely unexplored
- A. Cerebral specialization has been suggested to explain differences in verbal and spatial abilities—degree of localization of function
- B. Corpus callosum is larger in females than in males

V. Gender differences in personality from the different perspectives
- A. Psychoanalytic approaches
    1. In the psychoanalytic, differences arise from responses to structural differences (a biologically-based explanation)
- B. Neoanalytic approaches
    1. Erikson saw male traits (active, exploring) as tied to outward-extending genitalia; the female's nurturing and peaceful traits were tied to the internality of her genitalia
    2. Horney saw penis-envy as a small factor and described men's "womb envy"
        - a. women envied men's opportunities and roles, not their penises
    3. Jung believed that maleness and femaleness were both important
        - a. animus and anima
        - b. incorporate both (androgyny) for healthy personality

C. Biological/evolutionary approaches
    1. Successful reproduction requires different sexual behaviors of men and women
        a. men: many sexual contacts
        b. women: few, selective sexual contacts
    2. Animal research with the maternal instinct indicates a biological basis
D. Humanistic approaches: emphasize the good qualities that *any* self-actualized person would have, including
    1. Traditionally female empathy and openness
    2. Traditionally male creativity and autonomy
E. Social learning: gender differences are learned, reinforced behaviors
    1. Parents as primary socializers of sex-typed characteristics
    2. Other societal models, including the media, reinforce these lessons
F. Cognitive component: Gender schema theories
    1. Our culture and gender-role socialization provide us with gender schemas
    2. Schemas act as cognitive filters and are thus self-perpetuating
G. Trait approaches to masculinity and femininity
    1. Are these opposite poles of a single trait? Two independent dimensions?
        a. Bem Sex Role Inventory and androgyny
    2. Male-female differences have been studied in a variety of areas, including
        a. aggression and dominance
        b. emotionality
        c. achievement motivation
H. Interactionist approaches: Social and interpersonal characteristics
    1. Many gender relevant activities are closely tied to situational demands
        a. helping (gender differences in the types of help offered)
        b. nurturance/caring
        c. sociability
        d. nonverbal behaviors
        e. influenceability
        f. instrumentality vs. expressiveness
            i. Eagly's studies
I. Cross-cultural studies of gender differences indicate that many gender characteristicsare culturally determined
    1. Mead
    2. Oakley
    3. Whiting and Edwards

VI. Love and sexual behavior
   A. Stereotypes posit that men want sex, women want love
   B. Stereotypes of female sexuality throughout history are widely varying
   C. Culture provides context for learning "appropriate" sexual behaviors
      1. Double standards for men vs. women regarding infidelity and premarital sex emphasize the "men want sex" and "women want love" ideas
      2. Study of Boston college students showed men to be more romantic and to have more "love"; were also more devastated by loss of the relationship
   D. Human sexual behavior relatively uninfluenced by hormone levels

Classroom Activities, Discussion Topics and Projects

1. There are lots of books on the market which claim to "explain" the differences between men and women (for example, the hugely popular "Men are from Mars, Women are from Venus"). How much of male-female differences in such areas as communication can be explained by "personality"? How much is due to differing socialization of girls and boys, men and women?

2. Have students write down three ways that their parents socialized them to gender-related norms when they were children. How many of these habits still remain? Are they things that the students would like to be rid of? Do the students see that these gender-roles serve useful purposes? If they would like to be free of these norms, when did they first realize that this wasn't the way it "had to be"?

3. Discuss the curiosity, and perhaps discomfort, we feel when we cannot discern whether someone is male or female. Why is this so important to us?

4. Some experts advocate that parents should attempt to raise "gender-neutral" children—that is, the child should have all sorts of toys (trucks and dolls) and should be dressed in an androgynous way. Is it possible to raise a gender-neutral child in today's society? What are some of the barriers that a parent might encounter?

5. Discuss some of the male-female differences in the ways people act that, although behaviorally different, are functionally equivalent. For example, women have a greater tendency to use prescription drugs to deal with depression (this is less acceptable for men), whereas depressed men are more likely drink alcohol (a more socially acceptable way for them to deal with their problems). The outcomes are quite similar, but the substances used are different and have gender-related norms attached to them. How are people who "cross over" (that is, perform the non-normative behavior) stigmatized? If the outcomes are equivalent, why is this so?

Recommended Outside Readings

Gray, J. (1992). Men are from Mars, women are from Venus: A practical guide for improving communication and getting what you want in your relationships. New York: Harper Collins.

Buss, D. M. (1994). The evolution of desire: Strategies of human mating. New York: Basic Books.

Crichton, M. (1994). Disclosure. New York: Alfred A. Knopf.

Films / Videos

"Men and Women: Talking Together." Communication between the sexes is discussed by Deborah Tannen and Robert Bly, including an address of conversational rituals and the use of comforting as a power tool. The discussants take questions from a live audience. 58 minutes. 1993. Insight Media: 800-233-9910.

"Dear Lisa: A Letter to My Sister." This video includes interviews with 13 women from diverse backgrounds. They discuss the topics of sex-typed toys, women in the workplace, self esteem, and body image. 45 minutes. 1991. Insight Media: 800-233-9910.

"Man Oh Man: Growing Up Male in America." Looks at the ways in which societal pressures mold men's lives (includes interview segments). Addresses the issue of being "macho" and the related fears and feelings of vulnerability. 18 minutes. 1987. Insight Media: 800-233-9910.

"When Harry Met Sally." Story of a man and woman who become friends and eventually grow to love each other. This film nicely illustrates some of the communication problems men and women experience, as well as stereotypical male/female "personalities" and views on "love." 96 minutes. CastleRock Entertainment. 1989.

"Gender and Communication: She Talks, He Talks." Looks at the communication gap between the sexes. Also addresses the ways in which male/female communication differences may have developed. 22 minutes. 1994. Insight Media: 800-233-9910

"Men Are from Mars CD-ROM". Interactive seminar with author John Gray about communication between the sexes. 1996. Insight Media. www.insight-media.com

CHAPTER 12: STRESS, ADJUSTMENT, AND HEALTH DIFFERENCES

This chapter continues the section on "applications to individual differences," which shows how the theory and research of the eight basic perspectives can be applied to fascinating and important issues in science and society. In particular, chapter 12 focuses on healthy and unhealthy personalities, a popular topic of high interest to students.

Is it true that worriers get headaches, and repressed women get breast cancer? Are there general cancer-prone personalities and coronary-prone personalities? Are there self-healing personalities who manage to live a long and healthy life? This chapter examines the relations among personality, stress, adjustment, and health. By considering personality in an applied sphere like health, we are following the advice of Kurt Lewin, Gordon Allport, Sigmund Freud, Carl Rogers and other great theorists that the individual is best understood when studied in a real-world social context.

Possible Lecture Outline

I. Disease-prone personalities: How is personality linked to health?
- A. Health behaviors: What we do may promote disease
  1. Those with emotion-regulation problems might be more likely to smoke, drink, etc. in order to change physiological state and mood
  2. Social factors may influence some individuals to engage in unhealthy behaviors
  3. Certain "personality types" may be likely to seek out certain types of behaviors
     - a. Zuckerman's sensation seeking
     - b. Farley's Type T
- B. The sick role: Some people respond to stress by entering the sick role
  1. Sick role: societal expectations about how to behave when you're not healthy
  2. There are various rewards associated with the sick role (sympathy, paid work leave, etc.)
  3. Symptom perceptions are affected by attitudinal and attentional factors and thereby influenced by moods
- C. Disease-caused personality changes (somatopsychic effects): Genetic conditions and organic diseases can influence behaviors, moods, and personality

II. Diathesis-stress model of disease
   A. The idea that individuals have predispositions to various diseases or disorders, but that until the person undergoes stress, the disease/disorder will not occur; in the presence of stress it is this "weak link" that will give way
   B. Lown has created a model which attempts to explain important factors in sudden cardiac death; includes:
      1. Electrical instability
      2. Pervasive emotional state
      3. Triggering event
   C. Several studies have linked personality and health, but in complex ways
      1. Western Electric's study
      2. Stavraky's lung cancer study

III. Coronary-proneness
   A. Rosenman and Friedman's "Type A Behavior Pattern" describes a pattern of hostility, hurriedness, and tension; this was proposed to arouse the sympathetic nervous system and cause heart damage.
      1. Research has shown that the hostility and "struggle" are indeed harmful to health.
   B. Seligman's "Learned Helplessness" describes the situation in which someone learns that s/he cannot control his/her environment and so stops trying. This learned helplessness has also been shown to be related to health and longevity (although not just to heart problems).

IV. The Termites: Individuals studies since the 1920s, first by Lewis Terman, later by others.
   A. It was found that children who were more "conscientious" lied longer lives; they smoked and drank less and were less likely to have accidents, but this didn't completely explain the effect.
   B. Sociability, which is generally viewed as a "healthy" characteristic, was not related to better physical health outcomes.
   C. Children who were more "cheerful" died sooner; they smoked and drank more and took more risks, but this only partially explained the effect.
   D. The experience of parental divorce was found to predict earlier mortality; these individuals were more likely to have their own marriages end in divorce, but this did not completely explain the relationship.
   E. It was also found that males who experienced mental health problems or difficulties in adjustment were at an increased risk for early mortality.
   F. These findings from the Terman archives provide an exciting window on the interrelationship of personality and health; they also illustrate the complexity of such research-- there are no simple explanations for the personality-health relationship.

V. Blaming the victim
  A. The unfairness of placing too much responsibility on individuals for their illnesses
    1. It is psychologically appealing (reassuring) to assume you are different from those who are ill, so you will be protected from illness yourselves
    2. People want to believe in a predictable (cause and effect) world
  B. On the other hand, people must take personal responsibility for our health (instead of developing learned helplessness)

VI. Self-healing personalities
  A. Maddi and Kobasa's "hardiness" includes:
    1. Sense of being in control
    2. Commitment to life and work
    3. Seeing change as exciting and challenging
  B. Rotter's "Locus of Control" (feeling a sense of power in one's environment) and Trust
  C. There are two broad types of healthy personalities
    1. The "active" healthy personality: Functions optimally in a somewhat stressful environment; outgoing and spontaneous
    2. The "relaxed" healthy personality: Functions optimally in a low-stress environment; calm and philosophical
    3. The match between a person's basic style and the environment is important

VII. The influence of existential/humanistic psychology on understanding of self-healing
  A. Personality researchers have drawn from humanism and existentialism because they focus on positive human functioning
  B. Studying seriously ill, terminally ill, and survivors of terrible events provides a window on what makes one healthy, happy, and able to gain a sense of fulfillment in life
    1. Antonovsky's "Sense of Coherence" describes one's ability to find meaning in life-- to be purposeful. His theories attempt to shift the focus from illness to health.

Classroom Activities, Discussion Topics, and Projects

1. Have the students close their eyes while you take them through a 2-3 minute guided imagery sequence (standing on a ledge atop a skyscraper, or cutting and tasting a lemon are usually quite effective). Discuss the relationship between what's happening mentally and how this has a physiological effect (for instance, some students will be feel their heart racing when you take them to the edge of the "skyscraper" and some will salivate and pucker when they taste the "lemon"). Talk about individual differences in reactivity and how these might affect the stress-health relationship.

2. Discuss Type A Behavior Pattern as it was originally conceptualized and compare this with current conceptions of the construct. Have students role play the behavior patterns of Type A, Type B, and Type C. Have students identify which pattern best fits with their typical behaviors. Discuss implications for health.

3. Have students complete Zuckerman's Sensation Seeking Scale [Zuckerman, M., Eysenck, S., & Eysenck, H. J. (1978). Sensation seeking in England and America: Cross-cultural, age, and sex comparisons. Journal of Consulting and Clinical Psychology, 46, 139-149]. Discuss the concept of sensation seeking and its implications for health.

Recommended Outside Readings

Payer, L. (1996). Medicine and culture: Varieties of treatment in the United States, England, West Germany, and France. New York: Henry Holt.

Friedman, H. S., Tucker, J. S., Tomlinson-Keasey, C., Schwartz, J. E., Wingard, D. L., & Criqui, M. H. (1993). Does childhood personality predict longevity? Journal of Personality and Social Psychology, 65, 176-185.

Friedman, H. S., Tucker, J. S., Schwartz, J. E., Tomlinson-Keasey, C., Martin, L. R., Wingard, D. L., & Criqui, M. H. (1995). Psychosocial and behavioral predictors of longevity: The aging and death of the "Termites." American Psychologist, 50, 69-78.

Friedman, H. S., & Booth-Kewley, S. (1987). The "disease-prone personality": A meta-analytic view of the construct. American Psychologist, 42, 539-555.

Friedman, H. S. (1991). The self-healing personality: Why some people achieve health and others succumb to illness. New York: Henry Holt.

Kobasa, S. C. (1979). Stressful life events, personality, and health: An inquiry into hardiness. Journal of Personality and Social Psychology, 37, 1-11.

Films / Videos

"Getting a Handle on Stress." Looks at a stress evaluation (determining a person's reactivity). Explains effects of stress and stress management. 26 minutes. 1988. Films for the Humanities and Sciences: 800-257-5126.

"Discovering Psychology: Health, Mind, and Behavior." This video takes a look at the biopsychosocial model and compares it to the traditional medical model. 1990. 30 minutes. Annenberg/CPB Multimedia Collection: 800-532-7637.

"Health, Stress, and Coping." Looks at lots of different stressors and uses case studies to highlight the relationship between stress and illness. Has Norman Cousins discussing Selye's G.A.S. 30 minutes. 1985. Annenberg/CPB Multimedia Collection: 800-532-7637.

"The Psychobiology of Stress." Looks at brain controls on stress response via hormones, etc. 10 minutes. 1988. Insight Media: 800-233-9910.

"The Mind: Pain and Healing." Looks at the mind's role in pain and healing. 60 minutes. 1990. Annenberg/CPB Multimedia Collection: 800-532-7637.

CHAPTER 13: CULTURAL AND ETHNIC DIFFERENCES

Since culture is one key determinant of what it means to be a person, the systematic study of these cultural influences should be, as Allport and others noted, an essential part of personality psychology. Modern personality psychology should draw on its rich traditions of cultural awareness. These influences are the subject of this chapter. The emphasis is on science and logic rather than political correctness.

Although this whole chapter is a unique one, also noteworthy are considerations of socioeconomic status and of language. These matters fit nicely and are major topics in related fields, but are usually overlooked in personality psychology.

Possible Lecture Outline

I. Why is there a gap in knowledge about the ethnic and cultural aspects of personality?
   A. Laboratory studies are often not conducive to cross-cultural investigations
   B. There are relatively few professors from cultural minority groups
   C. Students tend to become researchers who follow the academic "tradition" of their mentors

II. Why is an understanding of culture important for an understanding of personality? Because personality development is influenced by:
   A. Family
   B. Peers
   C. Societal institutions (churches, schools, government, etc.)
   D. Ethnicity
   E. Class

III. History of research on personality and culture
   A. Mead's studies of Samoan society, especially the transitions of adolescence
   B. Whiting and Whiting's studies of childrearing in individualistic vs. collectivist societies
   C. Linton's influential book, The Cultural Background of Personality
   D. Lewin's studies of leadership and group dynamics in democratic vs. autocratic "societies"
   E. Distinction between emic (culture-specific) vs. etic (cross-cultural) approaches

IV. Errors of scientific inference: The case of race
   A. Humans form groups based on many different criteria
      1. Beliefs (such as religious or political)
      2. Customs (such as food, clothing, or music)
      3. Physical characteristics (such as skin color or facial features)
         a. because physical characteristics are so easy to notice, they are often over-used in assessing others "at a glance"
   B. The "American Dilemma" describes American lip-service to equality in the face of injustice based on physical characteristics
   C. Should personality psychologists study race?

V. Socioeconomic factors
   A. The SES gradient (those at higher SES are at lower risk of disease, premature death)
   B. SES effects on personality are not well documented
   C. The effects of economics on individual behavior have been studied (e.g. Marx and Fromm)

VI. Importance of language
   A. Language is an important aspect of one's identity
      1. Native language
      2. Dialect (regional variations)
      3. Idiolect (individual variations)
   B. Importance of language illustrated in the distinctive nature of the deaf "culture"; also in the passion some feel for the "English only" movement
   C. "Linguistic Relativity" posits that our interpretations of the world are greatly influenced by the language we use to describe the world
      1. Language can influence our social interactions in meaningful ways (e.g. we address powerful and important people in certain ways; the importance of these language rules varies by culture)
      2. Use of masculine pronouns as a generic for all people influences how we see the world, our own capabilities, and our roles (use of gendered language in general)

VII. Culture and testing
   A. Assumptions underlying psychological tests are sometimes biased
   B. Test scores can be affected by many factors
      1. Motivation
      2. Previous test-taking experience
      3. Qualities of the examiner
      4. SES
      5. Content may not capture cultural experience or may assume experiences not present

C. Researchers have attempted to create "culture free" and "culture fair" tests; other tests attempt to take culture into account
D. When are tests culturally biased and when do they indicate valid cultural differences?
   1. We need the framework of culture in order to appropriately interpret behavior and personality (e.g. Erikson's studies of the South Dakota Sioux)
   2. Culture influences the roles we select and thereby behavior (e.g. the health-promoting habits of Seventh Day Adventists); it therefore helps us understand the relationship between personality and health
   3. Cultural influences shape the theories we create to explain behavior and personality

VIII. Current research developments
   A. The nature of the self (independent vs. cooperative, as illustrated by Western vs. Eastern thought)
   B. The interactions of people with situations as impacted by culture

Classroom Activities, Discussion Topics, and Projects

1. Have students from several different cultural groups form a panel for discussion of normative behaviors and personality in their respective cultures. Allow the rest of the students to ask questions. Discuss how norms are formed and how norms may become so deeply ingrained that they seem almost "inherited."

2. Divide students into small groups to engage in conversations on a particular topic, but with language restrictions. For instance, you might ask them to talk about their romantic relationships without using any words related to feelings or emotions. This is useful for illustrating the importance of language in both communication and thought.

3. Discuss stereotypes related to the personalities of different cultural groups. Discuss the self-perpetuating nature of such stereotypes. What environmental factors might work to create such stereotypes in the first place?

Recommended Outside Readings

Allport, G. W. (1954). The nature of prejudice. Cambridge, MA: Addison-Wesley.

Jones, J. M. (1991). The politics of personality: Being black in America. In Black psychology (3rd ed.). (Reginald L. Jones, Ed.), Berkeley, CA: Cobb & Henry Publishers, p. 305-318.

Matsumoto, D. R. (1996). Culture and psychology. Pacific Grove, CA: Brooks/Cole.

Mead, M. (1963). Sex and temperament in three primitive societies. New York: Morrow. (Originally published in 1935.)

Films / Videos

"Valuing Diversity." Looks at how cultural differences get in the way of communication. Shows how body language contributes to communication, and how different cultures have different body languge norms. Addresses the dangers of stereotyping. 1994. 19 minutes. Insight Media: 800-233-9910.

"In My Country: An International Perspective on Gender." This is a 2-part series which addresses cross-cultural norms for household chores, discipline for boys vs. girls, marriage, control of money, care of elderly, and views of homosexuality. Interviews individuals from Mexico, Fiji, China, India, Japan, Lebanon, England, Taiwan, Sweden, Zaire, El Salvador, and St. Vincent. 1993. 91 minutes. Insight Media: 800-233-9910.

"The Eye of the Storm." Looks at a third-grade classroom (documentary) in which prejudice comes to life as students are divided into two groups: "brown eyes" and "blue eyes." Illustrates the problems that arise when too much value is placed on observable physical differences. 25 minutes. 1970. Insight Media: 800-233-9910.

"Higher Learning." Story of a group of freshman students who struggle with issues of ethnic diversity, identity, and sexuality. 126 minutes. Columbia Pictures. 1995.

CHAPTER 14: LOVE AND HATE

This innovative chapter is a student favorite, as it moves from serial killers and hate to love and attraction. It also serves to reinforce and elaborate the framework of various perspectives on personality. This chapter makes it clear that there is no simple, single explanation for personalities that love and personalities that hate, but we do know a lot.

As with other chapters in this book, this chapter shows the wider importance of studying personality, and gives many applications to daily life.

Possible Lecture Outline

I. The personality of hate-- how can we explain hate?
    A. Biological explanations
        1. Ethological explanations
            a. Hatred is innate because aggressive behavior was adaptive in our evolutionary history
            b. Natural aggression may be distorted and inappropriately expressed, e.g., Hitler
            c. Not very good at explaining individual and cross-cultural variations in aggression
        2. Brain disorders
            a. aggression and hatred may be prompted by structural (esp. temporal lobe) abnormalities
            b. aggression may be drug-induced (e.g. amphetamines, alcohol)
    B. Psychoanalytic and neo-analytic approaches
        1. Freud's "Thanatos" -- the drive toward death and self-destructive behavior which is unacceptable and therefore is projected or displaced
            a. example: anti-social personality disorder
        2. Jung's "shadow" archetype embodies primitive aggressive instincts; personality characteristics (such as thinking/extroverted) and certain complexes (such as a power complex) also help to explain hatred/aggression
        3. Adler focused on early social experiences, especially rejection which might lead one to see the world as hostile and to act accordingly
        4. Horney believed that when children feel unsafe they protect themselves with "neurotic trends," one of which is an aggressive personality
        5. Erikson believed that failure to successfully negotiate any of three ego crises might result in a hostile and hateful individual
            a. trust vs. mistrust
            b. autonomy vs. shame and doubt
            c. initiative vs. guilt

C. Non-biological explanations of hate
   1. Fromm emphasized the cultural milieu and the person's past experiences as sources of hostility and hatred
      a. our biology gives us a capacity for violence
      b. negative relationships with parents can work to create hostility
      c. most blame lies in our failure to find meaning in our increasingly advanced and impersonal society

D. Humanism
   1. Rogers believed that a lack of positive regard, especially from parents, results in negative emotions
   2. Maslow argued that unmet safety needs resulted in a neurotic passive-aggressive personality; the deficient environment causes the hatred

E. Hatred as a trait
   1. Cattell isolated source traits which, when present to an extreme degree, seem to characterize a killer
   2. Eysenck describes "psychoticism" as including impulsivity, cruelty, tough-mindedness, and anti-social behavior
   3. Feshbach saw anger as an emotional reaction that lead to aggression (altruism and empathy could counter aggression)

F. Cognitive approaches
   1. How we understand the world determines our actions (if we see a hostile world, we will lash out)
   2. Kelly described people with "cognitive simplicity" as making more coarse distinctions amongst stimuli; hostility results when we confront the unexpected

G. Learning
   1. Skinner argues that we have no aggressive tendencies; environmental factors cause the aggressive or hateful behavior
      a. classical conditioning theory would call hateful emotions "conditioned responses"
      b. operant conditioning theory emphasizes environmental reinforcements
      c. social learning theory incorporates the idea of learning hateful behavior through observation and modeling

H. Cultural differences in hatred
   1. There is evidence that there are a lot of inter-group differences in average level of hostility/aggression
   2. There are similar differences in how much hostility/aggression is deemed socially acceptable

II. The personality of love-- How can we explain love?
   A. Ethological explanations: love is innate because it was adaptive in our evolutionary history
      1. Evolutionary psychologists attempt to explain the differences in "love" for males and females using an evolutionary perspective
         a. males look for evidence of a healthy mate who can conceive and bear healthy young
         b. females look for evidence of health and the ability to provide for her and the offspring
      2. Are the observed differences due to gender roles? Cross-cultural studies suggest this is not the case
   B. Psychoanalytic and neo-analytic explanations for love
      1. Freud saw love as derived from sexual instincts; the strong feeling accompanying mature sexual attraction is "love"
      2. Klein saw the importance of the mother-child relationship because it provides the pattern for future loves
      3. Erikson saw mature love as developing in one's early twenties, during the stage of intimacy vs. isolation; if one doesn't have a true sense of identity at the outset, successful resolution of this stage is impossible
      4. Shaver described three styles of romantic attachment as modeled after childhood attachments
         a. secure lovers
         b. avoidant lovers
         c. anxious-ambivalent lovers
   C. Humanistic/existential perspective
      1. Those who have realized their potential are truly capable of love
      2. Rogers said children who learned to accept themselves would be capable of true love
      3. Maslow argued that love could be pursued only when physiological and safety needs were satisfied
         a. B-love (unselfish)
         b. D-love (selfish)
      4. Fromm saw love as one thing that actually makes us human; it's the result of our striving for contact with others
         a. immature vs. mature love
      5. May described five types of love; believed that love and will are intertwined
         a. sex (lust)
         b. Eros (procreative love)
         c. brotherly love
         d. devotion
         e. authentic love (combination of the previous four)

D. Cultural differences in love: there is evidence that there are a lot of societal and cultural differences in the expression of love
   1. arranged marriages
   2. attitudes toward premarital sex
E. Loneliness. Some characteristics of lonely people: difficulty trusting; difficulty talking about self;, less sociable; low on extroversion, agreeableness, and emotional stability; negative explanatory style
F. Love gone wrong: Violent or risky sexual behavior
   1. Risky behavior
      a. extroverts and impulsive people are more sexually adventurous
      b. psychoticism has been linked to sexual risk-taking (in fact, this is a core component of psychoticism, according to Eysenck)
   2. Violent behavior
      a. sexual aggression in males is predicted by various factors, including level of hostility toward women
      b. the "Attraction to Sexual Aggression Scale" is somewhat successful in identifying men prone to sexual violence against women

Classroom Activities, Discussion Topics, and Projects

1. Discuss whether or not individuals who have structural or chemical abnormalities in the brain which lead to violent behavior should be "excused." If behavior is truly outside someone's control, should they be held responsible for it? What should happen to people like this? What is fair? Ethical?

2. Have each student individually write down three to five instances from personal experience of events, objects, statements by other people, personal encounters, advertisements, etc. in which the student perceived a message that violence was a desirable or acceptable response. After the lists are finished, split the students into small groups to share their lists, and to discuss the relative prevalence of violent versus non-violent messages in contemporary society.

3. Discuss the issue of "quotas" for various types of disabilities. Who decides what a disability is? Who decides whether or not it interferes with the ability to perform a job well? What are the dangers inherent in NOT having any laws to protect those with disabilities? What are the inherent dangers in creating these types of laws?

4. Have small groups of students try to come up with well-known historical or fictional instances of relationships that exemplify each of Rollo May's five types of love. Sources can include myths, fairytales, bible stories, classical literature, modern literature, movies, television, current events—any source familiar to the students. After some time to come up with their lists, have each group share their examples with the class, describing why each example was selected.

Recommended Outside Readings

Herrnstein, R. J., & Murray, C. (1994). The bell curve: Intelligence and class structure in American life. New York: Free Press.

Lifton, R. J. (1986). The Nazi doctors: Medical killing and the psychology of genocide. New York: Basic Books.

Fromm, E. (1973). The anatomy of human destructiveness. New York: Fawcett Crest.

Films / Videos

"The Familiar Face of Love." Looks at how we choose mates and why. Illustrates that "falling in love" is not just a chance happening. 47 minutes. 1990. Filmmaker's Library: 212-808-4980

"The Wave." Shows a classroom experiment in which the teachers creates a "Reich" to show how the German people were drawn into the horrors of the Nazi regime. 46 minutes. 1984. Insight media: 800-233-9910.

"Schindler's List." Tells the story of how Oskar Schindler, a member of the Nazi party, saved more than 1,000 Jews from slaughter during WWII by employing them in his factory. Provides a good conversation starter on the topic of hate and whether, in fact, the propensity to hate is a personality characteristic or whether hateful acts are merely a result of environmental pressures. 197 minutes. MCA/Universal Pictures. 1993.

"The Case of the Hillside Strangler." Explores Kenneth Bianchi, a serial killer. BBC Production. 60 minutes. Also, "The Mask of Madness." Further exploration of Bianchi and his multiple personality defense. 60 minutes. 1997. Films for the Humanities and Social Sciences: 800-257-5126.

CHAPTER 15: WHERE WILL WE FIND PERSONALITY?

At the conclusion of the course, it is valuable to have students feel that they have learned something relevant and important. This way. they will be more likely to apply the lessons of different views of personality to ongoing issues in their lives, even long after they have forgotten the details of this course. To this end, it is useful to raise major personal and social issues.

What kind of world would it be if everyone had their brain chemistries continually adjusted or their behavior conditioned so that no one would yell at you, no one would rush to get ahead of you, no one would cry, and no one would worry whether she had turned the oven off? For every psychosocial problem, a pill or a therapist would be there. Even if such a world does not sound so appealing, the issues will not simply go away. We must be and remain educated about personality. Each perspective teaches us something valuable, but each has its flaws.

Possible Lecture Outline

I. Who studies personality? Who cares about what personality is?
- A. Gough's "psychological mindedness" scale of the CPI
  1. Interest in the needs, motives, and experiences of others
  2. Good judges of others' feelings
- B. Sometimes those with psychological problems are drawn to the study of psychology
- C. Demographics of personality and social psychologists
  1. Women
  2. Historically immigrants and members of minority groups

II. Brave new world of personality psychology: the coming developments that are likely to change the field of personality psychology dramatically
- A. Better understanding of brain biochemistry (the possibility of "designer personalities")
  1. Use of psychedelic substances such as peyote for hundreds of years
  2. Use of amphetamines, tranquilizers, etc. to treat mental problems
     a. Leary's experiments with LSD
  3. Use of "designer drugs" (such as Prozac) to alter personality
- B. More accurate societal control of environmental contingencies (resulting in better ability to control individual behavior)
  1. Thoreau's Walden vs. Skinner's Walden Two
  2. Behavioral shaping in schools, the workplace, and advertising
- C. Knowledge of the human genetic code may change our views of the genetic bases of personality

1. Cartesian dualism; knowing that the "mind" has a physical basis doesn't mean that the mind is simply biology
2. Genetics do affect brain and body development, therefore influencing some aspects of personality directly (such as by impacting activity level) and others indirectly (such as by impacting physical appearance which influences how we are treated and how we act in return)

III. The eight perspectives revisited
   A. Psychoanalytic, ego, cognitive, biological, behaviorist, trait, humanistic/existential, and interactionist
   B. Which perspective is most correct?
      1. The perspectives are really "philosophies" rather than testable theories, although some do yield testable hypotheses
      2. It's important to recognize the strengths and weaknesses of each perspective
   C. Should our goal be to merge all the perspectives? Should each person develop his/her own eclectic view of personality?

Classroom Activities, Discussion Topics, and Projects

1. With the increasing computer capabilities of the modern age, all sorts of information about each of us is constantly being gathered and stored. Our purchases, newspaper and magazine subscriptions, musical purchases, and frequently visited restaurants are recorded. What are the implications in terms of behavioral manipulation? How might knowing what we like/value/need allow others to control our behavior?

2. Just as many animals are bred to have certain characteristics, we may, at some point in the future, be faced with the ethical issues of genetically engineering people in the same way. With recent advances in cloning research, we are fast approaching this day. What are the ramifications of such science?

Recommended Outside Readings

Hogan, R., Johnson, J., & Briggs, S. (Eds.) (1997). Handbook of personality psychology. San Diego: Academic Press.

Kramer, P. D. (1993). Listening to Prozac. New York: Viking.

Pervin, L. A. (1985). Personality: Current controversies, issues, and directions. Annual Review of Psychology, 36, 83-114.

Pervin, L .A. (1990). Personality theory and research: Prospects for the future. In L .A. Pervin (Ed.), Handbook of personality theory and research. New York: Guilford.

SAMPLE SYLLABUS FOR A SEMESTER COURSE

Psychology 300: Personality

Required Text: Friedman, H. S. & Schustack, M. W. (1999). Personality: Classic Theories and Modern Research. Boston, MA: Allyn & Bacon.

The purpose of this course is to familiarize you with the major theories of personality, as well as current relevant research, and to aid in your understanding of their origins and the theorists who created them. In addition, I hope that by the end of this semester you will have answered for yourself the questions, "What is personality?" and "What determines personality?" As you will see, these are questions that countless philosophers and researchers have struggled to answer throughout time, and while there is no completely "correct" answer, there are some fundamentals that are generally accepted by psychologists today. To these basic tenets, you will add your own opinions and ideas-- perhaps based on the writings of new and innovative researchers, and perhaps based on your own creative thoughts!

You will find that most of the lecture portion of the class occurs on Mondays, and that quizzes and hands-on learning occur on Wednesdays. Be sure to read your chapters BEFORE the Monday lectures. On Mondays, listen carefully and take good notes; On Wednesdays come to class ready to discuss the previous period's lecture, test your memory with a quiz, and participate in an activity that will allow you to apply the knowledge you have achieved.

Grading: Grades for this course will be assigned based on a straight percentage of points obtained. *Make-up exams will be given and late work accepted* ***only*** *in cases of emergency and* ***only*** *with prior consent of the instructor.*

Assignments: Assignments and their point values are listed below.

Three midterms, 100 points each	=	300 points (30% of grade)
One Final exam, 300 points	=	300 points (30% of grade)
One Paper, 250 points	=	250 points (25% of grade)
Fifteen Quizzes, 10 points each	=	150 points (15% of grade)

Class Schedule

Readings will be discussed on the day they are listed.
It is your responsibility to read them BEFORE class.

Week 1	Mon:	Introduction to the class; textbook; syllabus; attendance; office hours.
	Wed:	Chapter 1 (What is Personality?); Quiz
Week 2	Mon:	Chapter 2 (How is Personality Studied and Assessed?)
	Wed:	Paper Assignment; In-Class Activity/Video; Quiz
Week 3	Mon:	Chapter 3 (Psychoanalytic Aspects)
	Wed:	In-Class Activity/Video; Quiz
Week 4	Mon:	Chapter 4 (Neo-Analytic and Ego Aspects); Quiz
	Wed:	Midterm 1
Week 5	Mon:	Chapter 5 (Biological Aspects);
	Wed:	In-Class Activity/Video; Quiz
Week 6	Mon:	Chapter 6 (Behaviorist and Learning Aspects)
	Wed:	In-Class Activity/Video; Quiz
Week 7	Mon:	Chapter 7 (Cognitive Aspects)
	Wed:	In-Class Activity/Video; Quiz
Week 8	Mon:	Chapter 8 (Trait and Skill Aspects); Quiz
	Wed:	Midterm 2
Week 9	Mon:	Chapter 9 (Humanistic and Existential Aspects)
	Wed:	In-Class Activity/Video; Quiz
Week 10	Mon:	Chapter 10 (Person-Situation Interactionist Aspects)
	Wed:	In-Class Activity/Video; Quiz
Week 11	Mon:	Chapter 11 (Male-Female Differences)
	Wed:	In-Class Activity/Video; Quiz
Week 12	Mon:	Chapter 12 (Stress, Adjustment, and Health Differences); Quiz
	Wed:	Midterm 3
Week 13	Mon:	Chapter 13 (Cultural and Ethnic Differences)
	Wed:	In-Class Activity/Video; Quiz
Week 14	Mon:	Chapter 14 (Love and Hate)
	Wed:	In-Class Activity/Video; Quiz
Week 15	Mon:	Chapter 15 (Where Will We Find Personality?); Quiz
	Wed:	Conclusion

SAMPLE SYLLABUS FOR A QUARTER COURSE

Psychology 300: Personality

Required Text: Friedman, H. S. & Schustack, M. W. (1999). Personality: Classic Theories and Modern Research. Boston, MA: Allyn & Bacon.

The purpose of this course is to familiarize you with the major theories of personality, as well as current relevant research, and to aid in your understanding of their origins and the theorists who created them. In addition, it is hoped that by the end of this quarter you will have answered for yourself the questions, "What is personality?" and "What determines personality?" As you will see, these are questions that countless philosophers and researchers have struggled to answer throughout time, and while there is no completely "correct" answer, there are some fundamentals that are generally accepted by psychologists today. To these basic tenets, you will add your own opinions and ideas-- perhaps based on the writings of new and innovative researchers, and perhaps based on your own creative thoughts!

Grading: Grades for this course will be assigned based on a straight percentage of points obtained. *Make-up exams will be given and late work accepted* ***only*** *in cases of emergency and* ***only*** *with prior consent of the instructor.*

Assignments: Assignments and their point values are listed below.

Two midterms, 100 points each	=	200 points (25% of grade)
One Final exam, 300 points	=	300 points (38% of grade)
One term Paper, 200 points	=	200 points (25% of grade)
Ten Quizzes, 10 points each	=	100 points (12% of grade)

Class Schedule

Readings will be discussed on the day they are listed.
It is your responsibility to read them BEFORE class.

Week 1	Mon: Introduction to the class; textbook; syllabus; attendance; office hours Wed: Chapter 1 (What is Personality?); Quiz
Week 2	Mon: Chapter 2 (How is Personality Studied?); Quiz Wed: Chapter 3 (Psychoanalytic Aspects); Paper Assignment
Week 3	Mon: Chapter 3, cont.; In-class Activity; Quiz Wed: Chapter 4 (Neo-Analytic Aspects); Quiz
Week 4	Mon: Midterm 1 Wed: Chapter 5 (Biological Aspects); In-Class Activity
Week 5	Mon: Chapter 6 (Behaviorist and Learning Aspects); Quiz Wed: Chapter 6, cont.; In-Class Activity
Week 6	Mon: Chapter 7 (Cognitive Aspects); Quiz Wed: Chapter 8 (Trait and Skill Aspects)
Week 7	Mon: Midterm 2 Wed: Chapter 9 (Humanistic and Existential Aspccts); In-Class Activity; Quiz
Week 8	Mon: Chapter 10 (Person-Situation Interactionist Aspects); Quiz Wed: Chapter 11 (Male-Female Differences); In-Class Activity; Quiz
Week 9	Mon: Chapter 12 (Stress, Adjustment, and Health Differences); Quiz Wed: Chapter 13 (Cultural and Ethnic Differences); In-Class Activity
Week 10	Mon: Chapter 14 (Love and Hate) Wed: Final Summary and Review

Sample Term Project I
Theory Integration

The purpose of this assignment is to help you think deeply about the psychological theories presented in class, and to allow you to integrate portions of these theories to create your own eclectic theory of personality. By piecing together segments of existing theories, you will get some creative, theory-building experience, without the time-involvement associated with traditional theory creation.

As we study different theories throughout the quarter, you should keep a record of the theoretical components that interest you in a notebook. This may be done in the form of a diary, lists of ideas, or whatever format is most personally useful-- the main idea is to create for yourself a pool of ideas from which to draw when you are ready to write your paper. This notebook will be collected and graded weekly, to give you feedback. The grades will be incorporated into your final grade for the paper.

The paper itself must provide an integration of ideas from at least three different theorists. These components may be large or small, and you are not limited to three. You may choose to use the ideas of one theorist as your main focus and integrate only small portions of other theories. Your paper must include the following: (1) a definition of personality, (2) a description of its markers (that is, how is it identified?), and (3) an outline of its developmental course.

Your paper should be between 10 and 15 pages in length and written following the guidelines of APA's Publication Manual. Papers will be graded on the following: (1) creativity of theory, (2) clarity of presentation, and adherence to all guidelines in the previous paragraph.

Sample Term Project II
Eight Perspectives on a Famous Personality

The purpose of this assignment is to give you experience in applying the theories you are learning about to a "real personality." You will begin by choosing an interesting person to study and analyze (be sure to choose someone you truly find interesting, since this person will be your focus throughout the course). You may choose any *public* person you like (a politician, movie star, musician, author, etc.), living or dead. The only requirement is that there *must be sufficient information* available about this person's life for you to adequately complete the assignment. Below is a short list of some interesting people whom you might want to consider; this is only a small sample, so be creative in your choice!

Woody Allen	Jim Morrison	Malcolm X	John F. Kennedy
Maya Angelou	Richard Nixon	Doris Day	Katherine Hepburn
Fidel Castro	Oliver North	Bill Cosby	Oprah Winfrey
Mohandas Gandhi	Pablo Picasso	Bill Gates	Michael Jackson
Shirley Temple	Elvis Presley	Bill Clinton	Woodrow Wilson
Elizabeth Taylor	Harry Truman	Adolf Hitler	Franklin D. Roosevelt
Princess Diana	Cesar Chavez	Eleanor Roosevelt	Simone de Beauvoir
Sigmund Freud	Abraham Lincoln	Jimmy Carter	Winston Churchill

Find a good biography or autobiography of this person and ~~a~~ read it. (If you can't find a book-length biography, you will have to choose someone else.) Supplement your reading with newspaper or magazine articles and interviews. Your goal is to get to "know" this person well so that you will have plenty of information upon which to base your analyses of his/her personality.

You will analyze this person from *each* of the eight major perspectives addressed in your textbook (in Chapters 3 through 10). One week after each perspective is covered in class, a 2-page analysis will be due, which will be graded and returned to you. For example, you will first analyze this person from Freudian perspective: What do you know about his/her childhood that would be of interest to a psychoanalyst? Does this person seem to be fixated at any stage? What are his/her personal relationships like? What conclusions can you draw? You do not have to **believe** every part of your analysis, but it must reflect the facts of the individual's life and the theory you are using.

After all eight perspectives have been read, discussed, and written about, you will combine your short papers into a final 10-15 page paper. This paper will be an integration of everything you have already written, incorporating the feedback you have received. A thorough and well-written analysis is expected. Papers should conform to APA style, including citation of all sources used (biographical and personality theory).

(Note to instructors: You may want to require students to get your approval of their chosen person. You may wish to allow fictional characters from literature.)

CHAPTER 1: WHAT IS PERSONALITY?

Multiple Choice Questions

1.1. How might personality psychology best be defined?
   a. scientific study of the way persons interact in social situations
   b. scientific study of what makes each of us unique
   c. scientific study of ways in which people are similar to animals
   d. scientific study of the theories of Sigmund Freud
   e. scientific study of what makes a person popular

   ANSWER: B
   DIFFICULTY LEVEL: M

1.2. Which of the following are accurate ways of assessing personality?
   a. physiognomy
   b. palm reading
   c. astrology
   d. face reading
   e. none of the above

   ANSWER: E
   DIFFICULTY LEVEL: E

1.3. Of the following, which is **not** a source of personality theory?
   a. analogy
   b. deduction
   c. conduction
   d. induction
   e. all of the above are sources of personality theory

   ANSWER: C
   DIFFICULTY LEVEL: M

1.4. Statistics are useful to personality psychologists because:
   a. they provide concise ways of stating relationships
   b. they are tools for understanding associations
   c. they help us to quantify large amounts of data
   d. all of the above
   e. they can help make vague theories sound scientific

   ANSWER: D
   DIFFICULTY LEVEL: M

1.5. Roots of personality psychology can be traced to the theater because
   a. actors often portray "characters" or easily recognizable types of people
   b. early studies utilized theater-goers as subjects (easily available)
   c. the early use of masks indicated fascination with the nature of individuals
   d. only a and c
   e. Shakespeare was Freud's best (most insightful) disciple

   ANSWER: D
   DIFFICULTY LEVEL: M

1.6. An early supporter of psychological testing (and where much testing is still conducted) was:
   a. large corporations
   b. the U.S. Armed Forces
   c. preschools
   d. nurseries
   e. existential flower power movement

   ANSWER: B
   DIFFICULTY LEVEL: M

1.7. Which of the following most emphasized the importance of life-span, longitudinal study of personality?
   a. Freud
   b. Allport
   c. Murray
   d. Lewin
   e. Kohler

   ANSWER: C
   DIFFICULTY LEVEL: C

1.8. If you read of a new "finding" in the newspaper one morning but noticed that only Caucasian subjects from Seattle were used in the experiment you might not give a lot of credibility to the study. This would be because of possible _________ confounds.
   a. cross-cultural
   b. gender-related
   c. computer nerd
   d. paranormal
   e. sexual

   ANSWER: A
   DIFFICULTY LEVEL: E

1.9. Advances in the field of biological science
a. have drawn attention away from the field of psychology
b. have helped researchers to think more clearly about what personality is
c. have demonstrated that there really is no such thing as personality
d. have enabled modern researchers to disprove all of Freud's theories
e. none of the above

ANSWER: B
DIFFICULTY LEVEL: M

1.10. Gestalt psychologists hold a fundamental belief that
a. life is what you make it
b. everyone is inherently good
c. people are more than the sum of their parts
d. all mental illness is rooted in childhood trauma
e. personality is static after the age of six

ANSWER: C
DIFFICULTY LEVEL: M

1.11. The Barnum Effect refers to the tendency to:
a. show off about one's good qualities
b. exploit the good qualities of others
c. view changing situations as a kind of circus
d. be conditioned through rewards and punishments
e. believe vague generalities about one's own personality

ANSWER: E
DIFFICULTY LEVEL: M

1.12. A nomothetic approach to personality:
a. seeks to formulate general laws
b. is the study of what makes each of us unique
c. studies ways in which people are similar to animals
d. involves the study of the "no mother" theories of S. Freud
e. studies pathetic aesthetics

ANSWER: A
DIFFICULTY LEVEL: M

1.13. If we ask everyone in the class to describe the personalities of everyone else they know in the class, and then use these data to form a theory about the personality of college students, we are using:
a. analogy
b. deduction
c. conduction
d. induction
e. reductio ad absurdum

ANSWER: D
DIFFICULTY LEVEL: M

1.14. A good theory is everything except:
a. comprehensive
b. parsimonious
c. falsifiable
d. tautological
e. productive

ANSWER: D
DIFFICULTY LEVEL: C

1.15. The roots of modern personality psychology can be traced to developments in the 19th century biological sciences based on the work of:
a. R. Descartes
b. C. Darwin
c. T. Roosevelt
d. I. Newton
e. M. Mead

ANSWER: B
DIFFICULTY LEVEL: M

1.16. Personality psychology that is focused on the study of individual cases is termed
a. idiographic
b. idiopathic
c. idiomatic
d. automatic
e. autopathic

ANSWER: A
DIFFICULTY LEVEL: M

1.17. When personality psychology uses the term "ego forces", this refers to
a. the desire to dominate others
b. the sense of identity or self
c. the need to focus on infantile needs
d. the need to maintain an inflated sense of self-worth
e. none of the above

ANSWER: B
DIFFICULTY LEVEL: M

1.18. A correlation coefficient is a mathematical index of
a. the degree to which one variable causes another
b. the degree of genetic relatedness of two family members
c. the degree of agreement (or association) between two measures
d. the degree to which values on one measure predict values on the other
e. Both c and d

ANSWER: E
DIFFICULTY LEVEL: C

1.19. When two personality measures are negatively correlated
a. low values on one correspond to low values on the other
b. the measures are most suitable for measuring negative traits
c. a high value on one measure is causally related to a low value on the other measure
d. the two measures reflect unrelated underlying traits
e. none of the above

ANSWER: E
DIFFICULTY LEVEL: C

1.20. The term temperament, as used in personality psychology, refers to
a. the extent to which an individual is moody or overly sensitive
b. the patterns of behavior that are considered appropriate within a cultural group
c. an individual's characteristic emotional and motivational nature
d. the extent to which an individual is warm vs. cool towards others
e. none of the above

ANSWER: C
DIFFICULTY LEVEL: M

1.21. The notion that there are personality "types", clusters of characteristics that tend to occur together
   a. cannot, in principle, be empirically tested
   b. is a very recent idea that first arose in the 20th century
   c. is central to a learning-theory perspective
   d. can be traced back to the ancient Greeks, at least
   e. none of the above

   ANSWER: D
   DIFFICULTY LEVEL: M

1.22. Darwin's evolutionary theory influenced the development of the field of personality psychology through
   a. the introduction of fossil evidence as a source of data
   b. the idea that people are subject to the laws of nature, like other animals
   c. its focus on divine intervention as a mechanism of population change
   d. its focus on how a species on an isolated island may differ from its mainland counterpart
   e. the idea that extinct populations can provide important data

   ANSWER: B
   DIFFICULTY LEVEL: C

1.23. Margaret Mead's view on the role of culture in personality was influenced by her findings from several different cultures that
   a. in some cultures, both the males and the females had the characteristics we identify as "masculine"
   b. in none of the cultures did the females have the characteristics we identify as "masculine"
   c. in every culture, the males had the characteristics we identify as "masculine"
   d. sexual aggressiveness is a dominant feature of behavior across cultures
   e. in every culture, strong maternal characteristics were seen in all women

   ANSWER: A
   DIFFICULTY LEVEL: M

1.24. With respect to unconscious forces, personality psychology as a field
a. ignores unconscious forces, focusing only on the conscious forces that people can describe and report
b. focuses on unconscious forces, because conscious forces are subject to bias in self-report
c. struggles to understand how and to what extent unconscious forces play a role in human behavior
d. has developed a clear understanding of the ways in which unconscious forces influence people
e. none of the above

ANSWER: C
DIFFICULTY LEVEL: M

1.25. An approach to personality would be called **nomothetic** if
a. it seeks to characterize the uniqueness of each individual
b. it emphasizes a historical perspective
c. it is based on detailed and reliable testing systems
d. it focuses on characterizing the life-course of individuals
e. it seeks to formulate laws that hold across individuals

ANSWER: E
DIFFICULTY LEVEL: C

1.26. If a theory is classified as "falsifiable", this means that the theory
a. has been shown to be false
b. could be claimed to be true based on misleading or counterfeit data
c. represents the null hypothesis
d. could be shown to be false by some type(s) of data
e. has been stolen from another researcher

ANSWER: D
DIFFICULTY LEVEL: M

Essay Questions

1.1. Describe one way in which religious beliefs and one way in which theater influenced the development of personality theory.

1.2. How does Darwin's theory of evolution help to explain the presence of personality characteristics?

1.3. Describe Margaret Mead's contribution to the field of personality psychology.

1.4. Discuss the sources of theories about personality.

CHAPTER 2: HOW IS PERSONALITY STUDIED AND ASSESSED?

Multiple Choice Questions

2.1. Reliability refers to:
   a. the ready availability of a scale
   b. the ability of a scale to give consistent results
   c. the ability of a scale to condense information
   d. all of the above
   e. none of the above

   ANSWER: B
   DIFFICULTY LEVEL: E

2.2. Random variation in measurement is termed:
   a. error of measurement
   b. validity
   c. error variance
   d. a and b
   e. a and c

   ANSWER: E
   DIFFICULTY LEVEL: M

2.3. A reliable personality test must have_______
   a. test-retest reliability
   b. internal consistency reliability
   c. a very large number of items
   d. both a and b
   e. both b and c

   ANSWER: D
   DIFFICULTY LEVEL: M

2.4. One way to address the "problem" that personalities tend to change to some degree over time is to:
- a. not measure it at all
- b. look for consistent patterns of response which indicate underlying personality stability
- c. always measure personality in the same situation
- d. don't measure personality until adulthood, when personality is more "set"
- e. none of the above

ANSWER: B
DIFFICULTY LEVEL: M

2.5. Validity refers to:
- a. whether obtained results are reliable over time
- b. whether the number of items on a scale is too large
- c. whether a test measures what it is supposed to
- d. all of the above
- e. none of the above

ANSWER: C
DIFFICULTY LEVEL: E

2.6. Discriminant validity is established when:
- a. a test fails to correlate with measures of unrelated constructs
- b. a test correlates with theoretically related constructs
- c. a test yields similar results over time and situation
- d. a test has items that correlate highly with one another
- e. a test has items that do not correlate with one another

ANSWER: A
DIFFICULTY LEVEL: M

2.7. When choosing items to include in a personality test, one wants items that:
a. correlate with other items in the scale
b. can discriminate between individuals with varying levels of the trait
c. are normally distributed
d. all of the above
e. none of the above

ANSWER: D
DIFFICULTY LEVEL: M

2.8. Wording of items is sometimes reversed to:
a. keep participants from becoming bored
b. save space on a questionnaire
c. determine whether those scoring the test are paying attention
d. avoid reversal errors
e. avoid response-set biases

ANSWER: E
DIFFICULTY LEVEL: M

2.9. Biases in testing may include:
a. gender bias
b. ethnic bias
c. cultural bias
d. all of the above
e. none of the above

ANSWER: D
DIFFICULTY LEVEL: E

2.10. The most common type of personality test is:
a. self-report
b. peer-rating
c. behavioral observation
d. structured interview
e. projective tests

ANSWER: A
DIFFICULTY LEVEL: M

2.11. Criterion-related item selection refers to:
a. selection of theoretically relevant items
b. selection of items that are most often endorsed
c. selection of items that discriminate among groups
d. all of the above
e. none of the above

ANSWER: C
DIFFICULTY LEVEL: M

2.12. Which of the following does NOT directly measure psychopathology?
a. Minnesota Multiphasic Personality Inventory
b. NEO Personality Inventory
c. Millon Clinical Multiaxial Inventory
d. all of the above measure psychopathology
e. none of the above measures psychopathology

ANSWER: B
DIFFICULTY LEVEL: C

2.13. Biological factors which may be related to personality are:
a. hormones
b. skull shape
c. levels of mercury or lead in the body
d. a and b
e. a and c

ANSWER: E
DIFFICULTY LEVEL: M

2.14. Which of the following are methods of assessing behavior?
a. sitting outside a market and watching to see when people open doors for one another
b. having people describe their beliefs on a particular topic
c. asking people what they typically do after dinner
d. having people wear beepers and write down what they are doing when they are paged
e. all except b

ANSWER: E
DIFFICULTY LEVEL: C

2.15. Because it may be difficult to assess the validity of a psychotherapeutic interview, which of the following is often used as the measure of validity?
a. the number of words the person uses when being interviewed
b. the amount of eye contact in the interview
c. the effectiveness of the therapeutic treatment (that is, the treatment outcome)
d. whether or not the person comes to the interview on time
e. the interview's correlation with the person's self-report of the problem

ANSWER: C
DIFFICULTY LEVEL: M

2.16. "Heidi is aggressive and extroverted." This statement describes Heidi in terms of:
a. types
b. traits
c. both types and traits
d. neither types nor traits
e. cannot be determined

ANSWER: B
DIFFICULTY LEVEL: M

2.17. One problem with using observable expressive behaviors as a method of personality assessment is that:
a. it is extremely easy to control expressive behaviors
b. most expressive behaviors are not observable
c. there is little variability in expressive style
d. expressive style is often strongly influenced by cultural and social norms
e. none of the above

ANSWER: D
DIFFICULTY LEVEL: M

2.18. If you were told that a child was taking a personality test and saw the child drawing a picture, the most likely conclusion would be that:
a. the child is distracted from his/her task, and so is unreliable
b. the child is completing a peer assessment
c. the child is taking a projective test
d. the child is being "warmed up" for the personality test ("pre-test")
e. the child is taking an expressiveness test

ANSWER: C
DIFFICULTY LEVEL: M

2.19. Projective tests do NOT include:
a. draw-a-person tests
b. inkblot tests
c. sentence completion tests
d. word associations
e. Minnesota Multiphasic Personality Inventory

ANSWER: E
DIFFICULTY LEVEL: M

2.20. Demographics include ________ and are useful in helping us to understand people's behaviors and personalities.

a. variables like age and religion
b. variables like the ability to concentrate
c. variables like level of extroversion
d. variables like motivation to succeed
e. variables like talkativeness

ANSWER: A
DIFFICULTY LEVEL: E

2.21. The Affective Communication Test (or ACT) measures:

a. High school achievement
b. A Comprehensive Testing of motivation
c. motivation to falsify
d. leaking of libido
e. personal charisma

ANSWER: E
DIFFICULTY LEVEL: M

2.22. Test retest reliability refers to:

a. temporal stability
b. the ability to concentrate
c. patterns of change
d. the success of a test to always measure the right (valid) concept
e. things that repeat, like talkativeness

ANSWER: A
DIFFICULTY LEVEL: M

2.23. If the assessment is not related to what it should not be related to, this is:
a. temporal stability
b. premature libido
c. very bad for validity
d. convergent validity
e. discriminant validity

ANSWER: E
DIFFICULTY LEVEL: M

2.24. When a person is given a stack of cards naming various characteristics and asked to sort them into piles on a dimension such as "least characteristic" to "most characteristic" of oneself, this is termed a:
a. sore sport
b. sport sort
c. P-sort
d. Q-sort
e. C-sort

ANSWER: D
DIFFICULTY LEVEL: E

2.25. The promising technique that can show brain activity by recording the brain's use of radioactive glucose is called:
a. EEG
b. galvanic skin response
c. Positron emission tomography
d. electron CAT
e. C-sort

ANSWER: C
DIFFICULTY LEVEL: M

2.26. The usefulness of projective measurement techniques derives from
a. their simple and reliable scoring methods
b. item response theory
c. the strength of the individual's defense mechanisms
d. their use of structured interview techniques
e. none of the above

ANSWER: E
DIFFICULTY LEVEL: M

2.27. Which personality perspective is most closely associated with the use of projective testing approaches?

a. psychoanalytic
b. trait
c. biological
d. interactionist
e. behaviorist

ANSWER: A
DIFFICULTY LEVEL: M

2.28 An important difference between projective techniques and self-report measures is in their reliance on

a. the willingness of the examinee to disclose personal information overtly
b. a standardized set of testing materials
c. the interpretation skills of the examiner
d. all of the above
e. a and c only

ANSWER: E
DIFFICULTY LEVEL: C

2.29. An "acquiescence response set" refers to the tendency of people filling out questionnaires to

a. have a bias to select the first answer option
b. have a bias toward saying "yes" to questions
c. select the answer option that they think the examiner expects
d. select the answer option that they think makes the best impression
e. agree to fill out questionnaires even when they would prefer not to

ANSWER: B
DIFFICULTY LEVEL: M

2.30. Which of the following approaches to the construction of a self-report test will eliminate or reduce the effect of the social desirability response set?
a. including many items that will be reverse coded
b. including items that have response options that are equal in social desirability
c. including an assurance that the scores will be kept confidential
d. including items that boost the self esteem of the examinee
e. none of the above

ANSWER: B
DIFFICULTY LEVEL: M

Essay Questions

2.1. What are the strengths and weaknesses of an objective approach to personality assessment? A subjective approach?

2.2. What is the difference between reliability and validity? Describe two ways of assessing reliability. Describe two ways of assessing validity.

2.3. Why do we want scale items to correlate with one another? And why should they not be *too* highly correlated?

2.4. Why would you want to word some questions on a test in the direction of the trait you are measuring (positively) and some in the opposite direction (negatively)?

2.5. What's the difference between an interview and a structured interview? What might be the advantages and disadvantages of each?

2.6. Briefly, what is the distinction between types and traits?

CHAPTER 3: PSYCHOANALYTIC ASPECTS

Multiple Choice Questions

3.1. Sigmund Freud was formally trained as a:
   a. mathematician and astronomer
   b. biologist and physician
   c. poet and archeologist
   d. magician and clinical psychologist
   e. pediatrician and physical therapist

ANSWER: B
DIFFICULTY LEVEL: M

3.2. "Hysteria," common in the 1800s, most often exhibited itself through the following symptom(s):
   a. intense itching and burning of the skin
   b. seizures and migraines
   c. uncontrollable verbal outbursts
   d. paralysis and functional anesthesias
   e. none of the above

ANSWER: D
DIFFICULTY LEVEL: M

3.3. Freudian theory would likely interpret a dream in which someone tries over and over (but fails) to scale a mountain to reach a friend, as indicating:
   a. secret lust for that friend
   b. jealousy toward that friend
   c. violent urges (to "knock off" that friend)
   d. fear for that friend's life
   e. fear of not being physically fit (body image)

ANSWER: A
DIFFICULTY LEVEL: C

3.4. According to Freudian theory, how might dreams be similar to icebergs?
- a. they are cold and impersonal
- b. a small part shows and much is hidden
- c. they are rare but beautiful
- d. examining them too closely is dangerous
- e. we underestimate our need to defend against them

ANSWER: B
DIFFICULTY LEVEL: M

3.5. The very core of personality, the id, has ______ as its main goal:
- a. to obtain pleasure
- b. to satisfy basic needs
- c. to solve problems/deal with constraints
- d. to keep the ego under control
- e. both a and b

ANSWER: E
DIFFICULTY LEVEL: C

3.6. The ego ________.
- a. looks for realistic ways to satisfy the id
- b. seeks pleasure at any cost
- c. operates on the "morality principle"
- d. is a Freudian synonym for "stuck-up"
- e. none of the above

ANSWER: A
DIFFICULTY LEVEL: C

3.7. The job of the superego is to:
- a. seek pleasure
- b. internalize the norms of society
- c. make the id more realistic
- d. put us in touch with our dreams
- e. all of the above

ANSWER: B
DIFFICULTY LEVEL: E

3.8. According to Freudians, why do "Freudian slips" occur more often when we are tired or distracted?
a. we get tired of consciously holding back true feelings
b. they don't occur more often-- we just remember them better
c. defenses are down and the unconscious slips out
d. we are more likely to daydream
e. none of the above

ANSWER: C
DIFFICULTY LEVEL: M

3.9. From Freud's perspective, a likely reason for someone to become fixated at the oral stage is:
2.10|F
a. he/she was weaned too early
b. he/she suffered a mouth injury that gave pleasure when it healed
c. he/she grew up in a home where everyone shouted
d. he/she was toilet trained too late
e. he/she grew up in a home where everyone talked a lot

ANSWER: A
DIFFICULTY LEVEL: M

3.10. Someone who is fixated at the anal stage might:
a. get a lot of pleasure from eating, drinking, smoking, etc.
b. be overly fastidious and neat
c. have passive-aggressive tendencies
d. both a and b
e. both b and c

ANSWER: E
DIFFICULTY LEVEL: C

3.11. A phobia is:
a. an irrational fear
b. theory based on dream imagery
c. the third stage of psychosexual development
d. an oedipal complex where snake envy is king
e. none of the above

ANSWER: A
DIFFICULTY LEVEL: E

3.12. According to Freud, male infants **first** develop attachment to _____, and female infants to _____.
   a. mother; father
   b. mother; mother
   c. father; father
   d. father; mother
   e. there is no consistent pattern

   ANSWER: B
   DIFFICULTY LEVEL: C

3.13. The period between the phallic and genital stages is called the _______ stage.
   a. electra
   b. latency
   c. parietal
   d. oedipal
   e. phallo intermediary

   ANSWER: B
   DIFFICULTY LEVEL: M

3.14. Freud believed that women in abusive relationships were there because:
   a. societal constraints kept them there
   b. they were seeking revenge
   c. they were fixated
   d. they were masochistic
   e. they were uneducated

   ANSWER: D
   DIFFICULTY LEVEL: C

3.15. The ego-protective defense mechanism in which traumatic events are forgotten is called:

a. repression
b. depression
c. reaction formation
d. projection
e. none of the above

ANSWER: A
DIFFICULTY LEVEL: M

3.16. A current controversy surrounding the idea of repression deals with:

a. people's failing to recover their repressed memories
b. vagueness of memories
c. implantation of false memories by therapists
d. masturbation
e. none of the above are current controversies

ANSWER: C
DIFFICULTY LEVEL: C

3.17. In Freud's time, many reports of childhood sexual molestation:

a. were followed up with court trials
b. resulted in the removal of the patients' children from them
c. were widely publicized, leading to a rise of the fascists
d. were thought to be imagined
e. caused only minor psychological trauma to the victims

ANSWER: D
DIFFICULTY LEVEL: M

3.18. Reaction formation is when:
a. painful memories are repressed
b. socially unacceptable urges are stifled
c. unacceptable urges are transformed into their "opposites"
d. for each regression there is an equal and opposite projection
e. none of the above

ANSWER: C
DIFFICULTY LEVEL: C

3.19. Rudy has unconscious urges to take things that are not his. He has never actually stolen anything, however. He works as a security guard at the mall and is very good at his job because he is very suspicious of others-- he sees evidence of thieves all around him. In fact, almost every time he sees an unfamiliar face, he believes the individual to be dishonest and looking for something to snatch. Rudy's ego-defense mechanism is:
a. repression
b. denial
c. regression
d. projection
e. none of the above

ANSWER: D
DIFFICULTY LEVEL: M

3.20. Jewel does not get along with her employer, and today she found out that she is going to be demoted next week. She didn't confront her boss; instead, when she got home, she yelled at her children and spanked her youngest child for a minor wrongdoing. Jewel's behavior is a classic example of:
a. sublimation
b. displacement
c. denial
d. regression
e. none of the above

ANSWER: B
DIFFICULTY LEVEL: M

3.21. Sublimation occurs when:
a. unhealthy urges are transformed into socially acceptable behaviors
b. dangerous memories are repressed
c. personal impulses are projected onto others
d. anal urges are turned into oral ones
e. none of the above

ANSWER: A
DIFFICULTY LEVEL: M

3.22. Regression in adults
a. does not exist
b. is a feature of normal development
c. is difficult to document
d. provides a creative and enjoyable recreational outlet
e. is much more common than in children

ANSWER: C
DIFFICULTY LEVEL: M

3.23. If Kathleen moves to another state (where her boyfriend also happens to reside) but she states that he had nothing to do with her decision, and that her only reason for moving is that she prefers the climate in the new state, she is most likely to be using _______ as an ego-defense mechanism.
a. rationalization
b. reaction formation
c. regression
d. sublimation
e. relational termination

ANSWER: A
DIFFICULTY LEVEL: M

3.24. Hypermnesia refers to when:
a. people forget large amounts of information quickly
b. people are unable to recall events from times when they were very physically active
c. detailed memories, previously only available in vague form, are recalled
d. all of the above
e. none of the above

ANSWER: D
DIFFICULTY LEVEL: C

3.25. One successful way of uncovering memories in psychoanalysis is:
a. sublimation
b. free association
c. sleep deprivation
d. all of the above are successful
e. none of the above are successful

ANSWER: B
DIFFICULTY LEVEL: M

3.26. When trying to recall which words, presented to you now, were on a list you saw previously, correctly identifying a previously-seen word is called a _______, while saying "yes" to a word you really hadn't seen before is called ______.
a. hit; miss
b. hit; false alarm
c. hit; correct rejection
d. false alarm; miss
e. correct alarm; correct rejection

ANSWER: B
DIFFICULTY LEVEL: C

3.27. Experimental research points to which of the following methods as being effective in aiding retrieval of memories?

a. hypnosis
b. free association
c. eliciting memories with relevant cues
d. a and b
e. b and c

ANSWER: E
DIFFICULTY LEVEL: C

3.28. If Steve plays an audiotape every night while he sleeps, to help him stop smoking, he is demonstrating his belief in:

a. subliminal perception
b. regression
c. infantile amnesia
d. all of the above
e. none of the above

ANSWER: A
DIFFICULTY LEVEL: E

3.29. Forgetting things you once knew is called _______ whereas the inability to create new memories is referred to as _______.

a. anterograde amnesia; retrograde amnesia
b. infantile amnesia; anterograde amnesia
c. retrograde amnesia; anterograde amnesia
d. retrograde amnesia; general amnesia
e. retrograde amnesia; hypermnesia

ANSWER: C
DIFFICULTY LEVEL: C

3.30. In his book Totem and Taboo, Freud traced the origin of civilization to the time when:
a. the penis became a symbol of uncivilized behavior
b. infantile amnesia characterizes adults
c. the first ape became lustful of his mother
d. faces were carved into religious poles (phallic like)
e. brothers came together and murdered the primal father of the tribe

ANSWER: E
DIFFICULTY LEVEL: C

3.31. Freud argued that the essence of personality was formed by the age of
a. twelve for girls, thirteen for boys
b. thirteen
c. ten
d. two
e. five

ANSWER: E
DIFFICULTY LEVEL: M

3.32. When Freud commented that "sometimes a cigar is just a cigar" he was referring to the fact that
a. cigars were believed to be less dangerous than cigarettes
b. he tended to interpret many long, pointy objects as phallic symbols
c. it was not a lack of ego-control that led men to smoke
d. women were not allowed to smoke because it was seen as masculine
e. dreamers with mental problems often smoked

ANSWER: B
DIFFICULTY LEVEL: E

3.33. Psychoanalysts would most likely predict which of the following outcomes in adulthood for a child who was severely punished every time he dirtied his diapers?
a. a tendency to save things, like a "pack-rat"
b. a tendency to be athletic ("run away")
c. a tendency to seek out many and varied sexual partners (dirty)
d. a tendency toward alcoholism (drown stress)
e. a tendency toward being overweight (full load)

ANSWER: A
DIFFICULTY LEVEL: M

3.34. The combination of a strong id and superego, along with a weak ego describes
a. the authoring personality
b. the autocratic personality
c. the aristocratic personality
d. the authoritarian personality
e. the androgynous personality

ANSWER: D
DIFFICULTY LEVEL: C

3.35. Which is not one of the five Freudian stages of psychosexual development
a. oral
b. anal
c. vaginal
d. phallic
e. latency

ANSWER: C
DIFFICULTY LEVEL: M

3.36. The fact that there are lots of jokes about and euphemisms for the penis supports
a. Freud's idea that repressed sexual drives underpin much of what we do;
b. Jung's notion of the phallus as the center of the collective unconscious
c. the notion of exaptation and adaptation as crucial tools of evolution
d. Skinner's notions of the ubiquitous peckering of pigeons.
e. Daly's theories of the sexual abuse of children.

ANSWER: A
DIFFICULTY LEVEL: E

3.37. In Freud's "Analysis of a Phobia in a Five-Year-Old Boy," Little Hans claimed to be afraid of....
a. heights and pointy mountains
b. his father's penis
c. snakes
d. horses
e. his step-mother

ANSWER: D
DIFFICULTY LEVEL: M

3.38. Which of the following are legitimate criticisms of Freud's "Analysis of a Phobia in a Five-Year-Old Boy"?
a. Because of his phobia, Little Hans was not a "normal child" and therefore his psychological characteristics are irrelevant to "normal" children
b. Because Hans' father, who supplied much of the data, was a friend of Freud and a close adherent to Freud's theory, the information he provided was probably biased
c. The investigation is limited because it was conducted on a Viennese child in the early part of the 20th century, and therefore may not accurately represent other people in other cultures in different eras
d. Both a and b
e. Both b and c

ANSWER: E
DIFFICULTY LEVEL: C

3.39. Freud attributed Little Hans' phobia of horses to...
a. Existential oral anxiety
b. Overcompensation for feelings of inferiority
c. Oedipal conflict
d. Erotic consciousness
e. Overdeveloped libido from excessive bathing

ANSWER: C
DIFFICULTY LEVEL: M

3.40. The job of the superego is to:
a. seek pleasure
b. internalize the norms of society
c. make the id more realistic
d. put us in touch with our dreams
e. assert superiority and self-confidence

ANSWER: B
DIFFICULTY LEVEL: M

3.41. When a televangelist like Jim Bakker passionately preaches religious morality in public while secretly engaging in immoral sex in private, this may be an example of which defense mechanism?
a. repression
b. denial
c. reaction formation
d. displacement
e. sublimation

ANSWER: C
DIFFICULTY LEVEL: C

3.42. Explaining great creativity like da Vinci's in terms of a re-direction of tremendous sexual energy reflects the process of
a. repression
b. denial
c. reaction formation
d. displacement
e. sublimation

ANSWER: E
DIFFICULTY LEVEL: C

3.43. According to Freud, penetration into the neurosis of a woman is likely to reveal:
a. Sexual love for her mother
b. Need for affiliation
c. A repressed tendency toward overcontrol due to fixation at the Oral stage of psychosexual development
d. A repressed wish to possess a penis
e. None of the above

ANSWER: D
DIFFICULTY LEVEL: C

3.44. A stressed woman who hides from her problems by climbing into her (older) husband's lap for comfort may be showing which defense mechanism?
a. sublimation
b. displacement
c. denial
d. regression
e. repression

ANSWER: D
DIFFICULTY LEVEL: M

3.45. Which trait is not associated with the anal character type?
a. orderliness
b. parsimony
c. dependency
d. obstinacy
e. inflexibility

ANSWER: C
DIFFICULTY LEVEL: C

Essay Questions

3.1. List the five stages of Freudian psychosexual development and briefly describe each.

3.2. What is the meaning of a "slip of the tongue" in psychoanalytic terms?

3.3. According to Freud, why would simply asking someone to tell you about his or her psychological problems be a poor method of assessment?

3.4. Describe either a) the Oedipal Complex or b) the Electra Complex. Include each of the following elements in your response: 1) the conflict; 2) the resulting fear; 3) the resolution.

3.5. How do the concepts of hits, misses, correct rejections, and false alarms relate to a patient who is undergoing psychoanalysis and is trying to retrieve memories? What are the associated rewards and penalties for each response, and how might these affect what happens in the therapy session?

3.6. Discuss the difference between the pleasure principle and the reality principle.

CHAPTER 4: NEO-ANALYTIC AND EGO ASPECTS: IDENTITY

Multiple Choice Questions

4.1. The term "neo-analytic" means
- a. lack of analysis
- b. lack of insight
- c. new analysis
- d. new anal stage
- e. new family

ANSWER: C
DIFFICULTY LEVEL: M

4.2. In childhood, Jung's ability to take the perspective of a rock
- a. caused him to be diagnosed as mentally ill
- b. suggested to him that he might have more than one form of being
- c. disturbed him
- d. all of the above
- e. was displacement of phallic imaginings

ANSWER: B
DIFFICULTY LEVEL: M

4.3. Jung believed that dreams and "visions"
- a. were things that no healthy person would have
- b. were foolish signs of an uncontrolled superego
- c. were indicators of psychiatric problems
- d. were important communications from another realm
- e. should be stopped with the use of moderate electric shocks to the head

ANSWER: D
DIFFICULTY LEVEL: M

4.4. Which of the following is NOT a division of the psyche according to Jung?
   a. the conscious ego
   b. the personal unconscious
   c. the paraconscious
   d. the collective unconscious
   e. none of the above

   ANSWER: C
   DIFFICULTY LEVEL: C

4.5. Jung believed the "mind" is comprised of ______ parts.
   a. two
   b. three
   c. four
   d. five
   e. six

   ANSWER: B
   DIFFICULTY LEVEL: M

4.6. Thoughts that Freud would term "preconscious" would fall into which of Jung's categories?
   a. collective unconscious
   b. personal unconscious
   c. general conscious
   d. collective conscious
   e. collective ego

   ANSWER: B
   DIFFICULTY LEVEL: M

4.7. Which of the following (bolded) thoughts/experiences might be found in the "personal unconscious"?
   a. Tracy does not think about her **grocery list** while she is doing a math problem
   b. Emery had a **fight with his girlfriend** yesterday, but when surfing he puts it out of his mind
   c. Neddie was **sexually abused** at the age of four, but has repressed the memory and doesn't seem to remember the incident at all
   d. all of the above
   e. none of the above

   ANSWER: D
   DIFFICULTY LEVEL: C

4.8. Archetypes are
   a. valuable archaeological artifacts
   b. powerful emotional symbols rooted in our human history
   c. patterns of emotion or temperament
   d. our beliefs about "god" as dictated by religion
   e. worthless copies of artifacts

ANSWER: B
DIFFICULTY LEVEL: M

4.9. The animus represents __________, while the anima represents __________.
   a. the male element of a woman; the female element of a man
   b. the female element of a man; the male element of a woman
   c. the male element of a woman; the animal element of a man
   d. the female element of a man; the animal element of a woman
   e. the animal element of a man; the animal element of a woman

ANSWER: A
DIFFICULTY LEVEL: M

4.10. Little Evelyn was caught stealing by her mother. As she tried to defend herself she said, "I didn't mean to do it-- my 'evil twin' took over." Evelyn is evoking the ________ archetype.
   a. anima
   b. mother
   c. shadow
   d. hero
   e. persona

ANSWER: C
DIFFICULTY LEVEL: M

4.11. A complex is
   a. a specific, strongly-held, religious belief
   b. a specific, strongly-held, belief about male-female differences
   c. a group of emotionally-charged thoughts & feelings about a topic
   d. a phenomenon in which sexual problems may be reversed through catharsis
   e. none of the above

ANSWER: C
DIFFICULTY LEVEL: M

4.12. Brian is struggling with himself. He's always been a good student, but lately his grades have been slipping a little bit. He feels like he has nothing in common with those who were once close friends, and yet he doesn't seem to "fit in" with any other crowd. He will be finishing his degree in history next year, but lately he's been wondering whether he really wants to be an historian (and he feels silly that he's wasted so much valuable time on something that he might not even want to do for the rest of his life). His girlfriend wants to get married after graduation, and he had planned to give her a ring over the Christmas break; but lately he's been feeling like marriage should wait-- he wants to have time to explore the world and "discover" himself before settling down. Brian seems to have

a. a superiority complex
b. an ecological crisis
c. an identity crisis
d. a generativity complex
e. a defeatist attitude (d-crisis)

ANSWER: C
DIFFICULTY LEVEL: M

4.13. Which of the following is NOT one of Jung's proposed ectopsychic functions?

a. sensing
b. thinking
c. feeling
d. intuiting
e. wishing

ANSWER: E
DIFFICULTY LEVEL: C

4.14. Jung believed there were _______ basic personality types.

a. four
b. eight
c. twelve
d. sixteen
e. twenty

ANSWER: B
DIFFICULTY LEVEL: M

4.15. Ken is a very outgoing person-- he makes friends easily, jokes with others, and is gullible (people love to play jokes on him because he is easily drawn into the game). Ken is also considered a good friend because he is a good listener and seems to truly feel what the other person is going through. Based on Jungian theory, Ken's seems to have a ________ personality.

a. feeling extroverted
b. wishing extroverted
c. intuiting introverted
d. thinking introverted
e. sensing extroverted

ANSWER: A
DIFFICULTY LEVEL: M

4.16. A superiority complex is often a reaction to

a. getting an A on an exam
b. being raised in a loving and supportive family
c. learning self-discipline
d. an inferiority complex
e. a lack of education

ANSWER: D
DIFFICULTY LEVEL: M

4.17. The concept of "masculine protest" describes

a. the desire of girls to be societally equal with boys
b. boys' protestations against being taught to "hold in" their emotions
c. individual striving for competence and independence
d. girls' desire to emulate their fathers rather than their mothers
e. lesbian liberation

ANSWER: C
DIFFICULTY LEVEL: C

4.18. Which of the following are among the social issues Adler believed everyone had to address?

a. societal tasks
b. occupational tasks
c. love tasks
d. all of the above
e. none of the above

ANSWER: D
DIFFICULTY LEVEL: C

4.19. Adler's typology was based on
a. the four Greek humors
b. Freud's id, ego, and superego
c. social interest and activity level
d. the four Greek humors and social interest/activity level
e. Freud's id / ego / superego and social interest / activity level

ANSWER: D
DIFFICULTY LEVEL: M

4.20. Horney believed that what women really wanted was
a. a penis
b. children
c. power
d. lots of sexual fulfillment
e. none of the above

ANSWER: C
DIFFICULTY LEVEL: M

4.21. Which of the following was NOT one of Horney's proposed styles of adapting to the world?
a. open style
b. passive style
c. aggressive style
d. withdrawn style
e. none of the above

ANSWER: A
DIFFICULTY LEVEL: C

4.22. To Horney, the goal of psychoanalysis was to
a. help the person achieve his/her "ideal self"
b. help the person to find his/her "despised self"
c. help the person accept his/her "real self"
d. all of the above, depending on orientation
e. none of the above

ANSWER: C
DIFFICULTY LEVEL: M

4.23. Patrice thinks she is a failure-- according to her assessment, her grades are bad, she is overweight, and she is unattractive. She also says she doesn't have any friends. In reality, Patrice does have friends, her grades are fine, and she is an attractive, albeit slightly plump, young woman. Horney would say that Patrice is over-identifying with

a. her despised self
b. her real self
c. her actual self
d. her ideal self
e. her negative self

ANSWER: A
DIFFICULTY LEVEL: M

4.24. Someone who is "moving toward" people would exhibit which of the following behaviors?

a. striving for power
b. seeking lots of recognition
c. withdrawal of emotion
d. all of the above
e. none of the above

ANSWER: E
DIFFICULTY LEVEL: C

4.25. Who has sometimes been called the "father of ego psychology"?

a. Freud
b. Hartmann
c. Horney
d. White
e. Jung

ANSWER: B
DIFFICULTY LEVEL: C

4.26. Who of the following was an object relations theorist?

a. Mozart
b. Jung
c. Adler
d. Hartmann
e. Mahler

ANSWER: E
DIFFICULTY LEVEL: C

4.27. Chris is two years old and well-adjusted. His attachment to his mother is healthy, and he is a happy child. Mahler would say that he is a _______ child.
a. symbiotic psychotic
b. symbiotic autistic
c. normal symbiotic
d. optimal symbiotic
e. symbiotic miotic

ANSWER: C
DIFFICULTY LEVEL: M

4.28. Who, in his therapy, often played the role of "therapist qua parent" in an attempt to help patients develop a healthy self-concept and overcome their narcissism?
a. Klein
b. Kohut
c. White
d. Hartmann
e. Erikson

ANSWER: B
DIFFICULTY LEVEL: C

4.29. Erikson believed that the first crisis an individual must struggle with is
a. identity vs. role confusion
b. industry vs. inferiority
c. autonomy vs. shame and doubt
d. initiative vs. guilt
e. trust vs. mistrust

ANSWER: E
DIFFICULTY LEVEL: M

4.30. Eunice is a retired book-keeper who, although she experienced no particular hardships in her life, is now miserable. As she looks back on her life she sees many things that she wishes she had done differently. For instance, she feels that she did not raise her children with very good moral values, and she also regrets that she did not pursue higher education (she often thought about it, but somehow things never worked out). Erikson would say that Eunice is experiencing the crisis of __________.

a. generativity vs. stagnation
b. ego integrity vs. despair
c. intimacy vs. isolation
d. identity vs. role confusion
e. initiative vs. guilt

ANSWER: A
DIFFICULTY LEVEL: C

4.31. Erikson's theory of development focuses on the idea that:

a. growth involves stages in which we resolve conflicts throughout life
b. increasing inner unity involves ego repression
c. trust vs. mistrust develops in adolescence and strongly affects adulthood
d. libidinal transformation is inferior to reinforcement
e. one must recognize his or her own feelings.

ANSWER: A
DIFFICULTY LEVEL: C

4.32. What is common to the following researchers: Emmons, Little, Cantor?

a. they all believe personality is fixed in childhood
b. they all study nonverbal behavior as a way of understanding personality
c. they all believe in a stage-theory approach to personality
d. they all look at people's goals as a way of understanding personality
e. all of the above

ANSWER: D
DIFFICULTY LEVEL: C

4.33. Jung claims that our ability to conceptualize certain types of individuals and experiences (e.g. evil spirits) easily is likely due to
a. the collective unconscious
b. our fertile imaginations (false truths)
c. the refractive unconscious
d. hallucinations experienced early in childhood
e. the personal unconscious

ANSWER: A
DIFFICULTY LEVEL: M

4.34. Who of the following has successfully negotiated Erikson's stage of Intimacy vs. Isolation?
a. Tom has lots of friends, but isn't yet too close to anyone.
b. Jill spends a lot of time alone and says she is lonely and depressed.
c. Anthony is thinking of getting engaged to be married but is cheating on his future fiancee; he says she doesn't understand him.
d. Nathan has a few close friends and just married the woman he has been dating for 4 years.
e. Elizabeth isn't sure who she is; with conflicting expectations from her parents and peers, it's hard for her to sort everything out.

ANSWER: D
DIFFICULTY LEVEL: C

4.35. According to Jung, the collective unconscious consists essentially of:
a. functions
b. archetypes
c. libido
d. complexes
e. functions

ANSWER: B
DIFFICULTY LEVEL: C

4.36. Karen Horney believed that women often felt inferior to men because:
a. they were experiencing penis envy
b. they were being realistic and knew they were inferior
c. they were raised to see men as superior, and society repressed them
d. they were focused on the collective unconscious idea of the Mother figure
e. she did not have an opinion on this topic, due to arguments by L. Hans.

ANSWER: C
DIFFICULTY LEVEL: M

4.37. The theorist who expanded psychoanalytic theory to include the life-span was:
   a. Adler
   b. Erikson
   c. Horney
   d. Cantor
   e. none of the above

ANSWER: B
DIFFICULTY LEVEL: C

4.38. The concept of "basic anxiety" was formed by which theorist?
   a. Freud
   b. Adler
   c. Horney
   d. Jung
   e. Funder

ANSWER: C
DIFFICULTY LEVEL: M

4.39. The stage at which an individual encounters the crisis of trust versus mistrust is:
   a. infancy
   b. middle childhood
   c. early adulthood
   d. middle adulthood
   e. old age

ANSWER: A
DIFFICULTY LEVEL: E

4.40. In neo-analytic theory, a child's fear of being alone, helpless, and insecure, which arises from problems in relations with one's parents (such a lack of warmth), is termed:
   a. basic anxiety
   b. inflexibile locus of control
   c. learned helplessess
   d. temperamental sensitivity (reticular system)
   e. anal mistrust

ANSWER: A
DIFFICULTY LEVEL: M

4.41. According to Erikson, healthy development results in an increase in the capacity for an individual to:
a. Do well according to his own standards
b. Do well according to those who are significant to him
c. Do well in acquiring and retaining desired possessions
d. Remain free of neuroses and conflicts
e. Both a and b

ANSWER: A
DIFFICULTY LEVEL: C

4.42. Although neo-analytic psychologists base their theories on psychoanalytic theory, they differ from psychoanalytic theory in the following way(s):
a. they are more interested in the "self" and in the social environment
b. they place less importance on developmental influences
c. they all hold central the idea of the collective unconscious
d. a and b
e. all of the above

ANSWER: A
DIFFICULTY LEVEL: M

Essay Questions

4.1. Describe Jung's idea of the collective unconscious (what is it, where does it come from, what is its purpose?). How does this idea of Jung's fit with modern personality theory?

4.2. Describe Horney's rejection of Freud's idea of penis envy. What was her alternative explanation?

4.3. Briefly describe object relations theories. How are they different from traditional psychoanalytic theory? What do they have in common with psychoanalytic theory?

4.4. List and briefly describe Erikson's eight stages of development. Choose one and describe what would happen if this crisis was not successfully negotiated.

4.5. What does it mean to say that Erikson "emphasized a balanced outcome as optimal for each of these eight ego crises"?

4.6. What is a "functionalist" approach to personality? How would a researcher like Snyder go about studying your personality and identity?

CHAPTER 5: BIOLOGICAL ASPECTS

Multiple Choice Questions

5.1. "Temperament" refers to:
  a. physical characteristics which correlate with behaviors
  b. individuals' widely varying fluctuations in mood
  c. stable individual differences in emotional reactivity
  d. the trait of being irritable and temperamental
  e. none of the above

ANSWER: C
DIFFICULTY LEVEL: M

5.2. Of the following, which are among the four basic aspects of temperament?
  a. activity, emotionality, and gender congruence
  b. activity and gender congruence
  c. activity and emotionality
  d. emotionality and gender congruence
  e. activity, emotionality, gender congruence, and vocalization

ANSWER: C
DIFFICULTY LEVEL: C

5.3. In what way does Eysenck link his dimension of introversion to biology?
  a. introverts are innately at a higher level of central nervous system arousal
  b. introverts are innately at a lower level of central nervous system arousal
  c. he doesn't specify a link
  d. introverts are either very high or very low in terms of central nervous system arousal
  e. none of the above

ANSWER: A
DIFFICULTY LEVEL: M

5.4. According to Eysenck's theory, an extrovert, if exposed to annoying external stimuli, would:
   a. be more bothered by it than would an introvert
   b. be less bothered by it than would an introvert
   c. would start out by being more bothered, and then become equal with, an introvert
   d. trigger an oedipal reaction
   e. none of the above

   ANSWER: B
   DIFFICULTY LEVEL: M

5.5. If personality has a biologically-based component, we should :
   a. find some personality "traits" cross-culturally
   b. find a single gene that completely accounts for a trait and its corresponding behavior
   c. see more personality similarities in monozygotic twins than in dizygotic twins
   d. both a and c
   e. all of the above

   ANSWER: D
   DIFFICULTY LEVEL: C

5.6. One of the first scientists to explore possible genetic links for personality, who tried to separate the effects of genetics and environment by looking at adopted twins, and who began the eugenics movement, was named __________.
   a. Charles Darwin
   b. Ivan Pavlov
   c. Francis Galton
   d. Hans Eysenck
   e. Floyd Allport

   ANSWER: C
   DIFFICULTY LEVEL: M

5.7. Biology might affect personality in which of the following ways?
a. physical characteristics affect the way others treat us, thus shaping our personalities
b. a child with a difficult temperament might be treated harshly by parents, thus shaping his or her personality
c. biological predispositions might cause some people to place themselves in stressful situations, and the experience of much stress may mold personality
d. all of the above
e. none of the above

ANSWER: D
DIFFICULTY LEVEL: M

5.8. The Cinderella phenomenon describes:
a. the tendency for stepchildren to be more physically attractive than biological children
b. the tendency for girls to be more affected, in terms of personality, by their looks
c. the tendency for biological children to be treated better than stepchildren
d. the assertion that a dream is wish your heart makes
e. none of the above describe the Cinderella phenomenon

ANSWER: C
DIFFICULTY LEVEL: M

5.9. Locke's idea of "tabula rasa" implies that
a. everyone is born with a "blank slate" upon which personality is stamped by life experiences
b. individuals are born with "habits" that are inherited from their parents
c. some individuals are born with innate skills, while others are learn these skills later
d. all of the above
e. none of the above

ANSWER: A
DIFFICULTY LEVEL: E

5.10. How does the case of Angelman syndrome demonstrate a genetic influence on personality?

a. people with Angelman syndrome are usually depressed and have an inactive temperament
b. people with Angelman syndrome are almost always happy, and are good-looking, but also walk jerkily and suffer from mental retardation
c. people with Angelman syndrome usually develop hostile personalities later in life
d. people with Angelman syndrome have a very flat affect-- basically no personality
e. none of the above

ANSWER: B
DIFFICULTY LEVEL: M

5.11. What does a "lie detector" have to do with Eysenck's biological theory of temperament?

a. Eysenck has found that extroverts are more likely to lie than introverts
b. it shows that there are no differences in lying behavior between introverts and extroverts, therefore biological underpinnings of personality are unlikely
c. it has nothing to do with Eysenck's theory
d. it can be used to measure levels of physiological arousal in people, and Eysenck posits that introverts are more physiologically aroused at baseline
e. it can be used to accurately place people into four discrete categories of temperament amongst which there is no overlap

ANSWER: D
DIFFICULTY LEVEL: C

5.12. Which of the following is NOT characteristic of Zuckerman's "sensation seeking"?

a. seeking out highly stimulating activities
b. preferences for large crowds of people
c. seeking out novel experiences
d. willingness to try new things
e. tendency to actively engage environments

ANSWER: B
DIFFICULTY LEVEL: M

5.13. Which of the following might link biology to personality?
   a. temperament is genetically programmed, and is a personality precursor
   b. our looks might influence how others treat us and thus how our personalities form
   c. temperament influences the environments we choose, and thus the experiences that mold us
   d. all of the above
   e. none of the above

   ANSWER: D
   DIFFICULTY LEVEL: M

5.14. In regard to the biological determination of homosexuality,
   a. some structural differences have been found when comparing the brains of homosexual with heterosexual men
   b. there are no differences between the concordance levels of monozygotic versus dizygotic twins in the occurrence of homosexuality
   c. there is no evidence that sexual orientation is influenced by biological factors
   d. it is clear that sexual orientation is completely biologically determined
   e. none of the above

   ANSWER: A
   DIFFICULTY LEVEL: M

5.15. One possible way that homosexuality might have been selected for evolutionarily is
   a. selective attrition
   b. evolutionary sublimation
   c. kin selection
   d. multiplicative evolution
   e. open selection

   ANSWER: C
   DIFFICULTY LEVEL: E

5.16. Where did the phrase "mad as a hatter" come from?
a. people wore hats in the 1800s to signify mental illness
b. Lewis Carroll coined the term in his "Alice in Wonderland" and it has been used ever since
c. hat makers were poisoned by mercury in hat factories and madness was a symptom
d. hat makers were notorious in old England for their angry and violent tempers
e. hatters faced periodic depressions due to changing fads and so were notoriously angry

ANSWER: C
DIFFICULTY LEVEL: E

5.17. Which of the following can affect observable personality?
a. poisoning by metals, including mercury, manganese, and lead
b. Alzheimer's disease, Parkinson's disease, and strokes
c. use of legal drugs (e.g. Halcion) or illegal drugs (e.g. LSD)
d. major surgeries, such as coronary artery bypass surgery (CABG)
e. all of the above

ANSWER: E
DIFFICULTY LEVEL: M

5.18. The textbook argues that there should be a field of study called "personality toxicology" which would mean that
a. experts would study "toxic" or maladaptive personalities
b. experts would study the effects of environmental toxins on personality
c. experts would study personality precursors to illegal drug use
d. experts would study the factors necessary for one to deal with stress
e. experts would study "toxic" or maladaptive interpersonal relationships

ANSWER: B
DIFFICULTY LEVEL: M

5.19. Which of the following is NOT an example of someone actively creating an environment?

a. John chooses to play competitive sports despite the fact that he sometimes gets injured because he loves the adrenaline rush and the cheers of the crowd
b. John picks his friends carefully because he doesn't want to hang around with people who are always getting into trouble
c. John was born into a large family and he likes this because he has lots of siblings to play with, study with, and talk with
d. John spends every Sunday with his grandmother because he enjoys hearing her tell stories of the "old days"
e. John broke up with his girlfriend because he felt their goals in life were too dissimilar

ANSWER: C
DIFFICULTY LEVEL: M

5.20. Kretschmer, the first to systematically study the relationship between physical appearance and personality, believed that

a. schizophrenics were more likely to be overweight
b. schizophrenics were more likely to be unattractive
c. schizophrenics were more likely to be attractive
d. schizophrenics were more likely to be thin
e. schizophrenics were more likely to have blue eyes

ANSWER: D
DIFFICULTY LEVEL: M

5.21. Which of the following is a correct match between Sheldon's somatotype and its description?

a. ectomorphs: plump and jolly
b. endomorphs: muscular and athletic
c. mesomorphs: plump and jolly
d. ectomorphs: thin and studious
e. endomorphs: thin and studious

ANSWER: D
DIFFICULTY LEVEL: M

5.22. Why might victims of serious burns of other disfiguring ailments tend to be shy?
a. others might avoid them, thus they have fewer opportunities to interact and practice their social skills
b. these types of ailments (burns, etc.) often damage brain tissue, resulting in shyness
c. these individuals are afraid to go into the world because they are afraid they will experience some great physical catastrophe
d. all of the above
e. none of the above

ANSWER: A
DIFFICULTY LEVEL: C

5.23. Research has shown that, in general, physically attractive people are assumed to be
a. more musically inclined than their less attractive peers
b. kinder and more successful than their less attractive peers
c. less athletic than their less attractive peers
d. less emotionally stable than their less attractive peers
e. none of the above

ANSWER: B
DIFFICULTY LEVEL: E

5.24. Social Darwinism supports the notion that
a. Darwin was a socialist
b. "superior" societies have the right to invade and conquer "lesser" societies
c. our social interactions are constantly evolving in an evolution-like process
d. the roots of social psychology may be traced to the writings of Darwin
e. Darwinian theory is most applicable to socialist societies

ANSWER: B
DIFFICULTY LEVEL: C

5.25. Sociobiologists
a. study how childhood affects later psychological functioning
b. study the rate at which children from different ethnicities learn
c. study the influence of evolutionary biology on social behaviors
d. study the biological predisposition to socialism
e. none of the above

ANSWER: C
DIFFICULTY LEVEL: M

5.26. In the United States, women could not graduate from top colleges such as Yale and Princeton until the
a. 1920's
b. 1940's (war years)
c. 1950's
d. 1960's
e. 1970's

ANSWER: E
DIFFICULTY LEVEL: M

5.27. A major study done at the University of Minnesota, studying identical twins raised apart has found:
a. impressive similarities in personality between people who have the same genetic make-up
b. similarities in physical appearance but not personality
c. personality is mostly located in the genes, regardless of the environment
d. same sex and opposite sex twins have similar personalities
e. people raised in Minnesota do not like Mexican food

ANSWER: A
DIFFICULTY LEVEL: C

5.28. Jenny is not a particularly happy toddler. She is easily frightened, and seems to be easily irritated. Her mother reports that she's not a lot of trouble, however, as she spends most of her time playing quietly by herself or watching TV; in fact her mother often has to encourage her to play with the other children in her day-care group. Describe Jenny on each of the following temperamental dimensions: 1) activity; 2) emotionality; 3) sociability.

a. low; low; low
b. high; low; low
c. low; high; low
d. low; low; high
e. low; high; high

ANSWER: C
DIFFICULTY LEVEL: C

5.29. Which of the following arguments points to non-biological factors in the incidence of schizophrenia?

a. many identical twins of schizophrenics do not develop the disease
b. individuals with schizophrenia often have larger ventricles in the brain
c. schizophrenics often show signs of brain atrophy or developmental failure
d. schizophrenia tends to run in families
e. there is controversy over the concordance rate for schizophrenia among twins

ANSWER: A
DIFFICULTY LEVEL: M

5.30. Biological factors which probably are related to personality are:

a. hormones
b. chromosomes
c. levels of mercury or lead in the body
d. central nervous system arousal level
e. all of the above

ANSWER: E
DIFFICULTY LEVEL: M

5.31. If we postulate that introverts are innately at a higher level of central nervous system arousal, this is an interpretation of:

a. Eysenck's linking of the dimension of introversion to biology
b. Pavlov's theory of the classical conditioning of traits
c. Freud's theory of the hydraulic nature of the id
d. Buss's theory of the evolution of less attractive men
e. none of the above

ANSWER: A
DIFFICULTY LEVEL: M

5.32. Daly and Wilson suggest that family violence and abuse against children in modern America is often due to...

a. Reinforced behavioral patterns that include violent actions
b. Psychological conflicts in the abuser's unconscious
c. Evolutionary pressures driving individuals to protect the human race from attack
d. Evolutionary pressures driving individuals to protect themselves against all others (self-preservation instinct)
e. Evolutionary pressures driving individuals to care more for their own offspring than for others

ANSWER: E
DIFFICULTY LEVEL: M

Essay Questions

5.1. What are some of the problems encountered in trying to test a nervous-system-based theory of temperament? Describe how electrodermal measures and electroencephalographs may be used to provide support for Eysenck's biologically-based model of temperament/personality.

5.2. How might the finding that identical twins are more similar to one another than are fraternal twins be explained with something other than a biological explanation?

5.3. If there is not a gene for "talented athlete" why might we expect that if one monozygotic twin is a high school football star, his twin brother might also be quite good at athletics?

5.4. How are evolutionary-selection explanations for homosexuality and for altruism similar?

5.5. In the textbook a number of environmental factors which seem to affect personality are listed. Name and describe three of them.

5.6. What is one way in which our "biology" may influence the types of experiences we have?

5.7. List and briefly describe Sheldon's three somatotypes. Why has this approach to 5.assessing personality become unpopular?

5.8. When sociobiologists apply their theories to humans, which three human social behaviors are most often used? Why?

5.9. What is the "Human Genome Project"? How is it different from the eugenics movement? How is it similar?

CHAPTER 6: BEHAVIORIST AND LEARNING ASPECTS

Multiple Choice Questions

6.1. In Pavlov's early classical conditioning experiments, food was the ________, and a bell which was originally a neutral stimulus became a ________ when paired with the food.

a. conditioned stimulus; unconditioned stimulus
b. conditioned stimulus; unconditioned response
c. unconditioned stimulus; unconditioned response
d. unconditioned stimulus; conditioned stimulus
e. unconditioned stimulus; conditioned response

ANSWER: D
DIFFICULTY LEVEL: M

6.2. In the following scenario, what is the conditioned stimulus? "Miles is an extremely smart dog. His owner always feeds him dog food from a can, which the owner opens using an electric can-opener. Whenever Miles hears the sound of the electric can opener, he runs into the kitchen and over to his food bowl."

a. the can of dog food
b. the food bowl
c. the sound of the can opener
d. running to the food bowl
e. all of the above

ANSWER: C
DIFFICULTY LEVEL: M

6.3. When a conditioned response occurs in response to a stimulus that is similar to the conditioned stimulus, this is called

a. generalization
b. discrimination
c. reaction
d. optimization
e. lateralization

ANSWER: A
DIFFICULTY LEVEL: E

6.4. When an individual is able to discern that a given stimulus is NOT the conditioned stimulus, and therefore does not perform the conditioned response, this is called
a. generalization
b. discrimination
c. reaction
d. optimization
e. lateralization

ANSWER: B
DIFFICULTY LEVEL: M

6.5. From the behaviorist perspective, the term "extinction" refers to
a. a species of animal dying out
b. someone holding back from doing a behavior that s/he really wants to do
c. a "dying out" of a conditioned response when it is no longer paired with an unconditioned stimulus
d. all of the above
e. none of the above

ANSWER: C
DIFFICULTY LEVEL: E

6.6. In the dogs that he worked with, Pavlov was able to classically condition something similar to which personality dimension?
a. agreeableness
b. openness
c. friendliness
d. neuroticism
e. conscientiousness

ANSWER: D
DIFFICULTY LEVEL: M

6.7. The behaviorist movement was born in reaction to what practice of psychology
a. subjective analyses and introspection
b. physiological measurement
c. Skinnerian principles of learning
d. all of the above
e. none of the above

ANSWER: A
DIFFICULTY LEVEL: M

6.8. After little Albert was conditioned to fear the rat, he
- a. cried at the sight of a rat
- b. was also afraid of other furry objects like a rabbit and a fur coat
- c. demonstrated an emotional reaction to a formerly neutral/positive stimulus (the rat)
- d. all of the above
- e. none of the above

ANSWER: D
DIFFICULTY LEVEL: M

6.9. When Jones extinguished Peter's fear of the rabbit by gradually bringing it closer and closer while keeping Peter happy and relaxed, he demonstrated
- a. classical conditioning
- b. generalization
- c. discrimination
- d. flooding
- e. systematic desensitization

ANSWER: E
DIFFICULTY LEVEL: M

6.10. Who developed & expanded the concept of "operant conditioning"?
- a. Pavlov
- b. Watson
- c. Thorndike
- d. Skinner
- e. Miller

ANSWER: D
DIFFICULTY LEVEL: M

6.11. The central idea behind the concept of operant conditioning is that
- a. behavior is changed by its consequences
- b. classical conditioning works best when a single individual does the conditioning
- c. behavior can be encouraged, but it cannot be discouraged
- d. once a behavior is learned it can never be truly extinguished
- e. behavior functions parallel to consequences, but is not influenced by them

ANSWER: A
DIFFICULTY LEVEL: M

6.12. Skinner's novel, Walden Two, describes

a. a peaceful and idyllic life in a cabin on Walden Pond
b. a life in which self-reliance is of paramount importance, and independence abounds
c. a utopian community which operates on the principles of operant conditioning
d. individuals fighting the government for their freedom
e. a theoretical argument that although environments condition us, we are still free

ANSWER: C
DIFFICULTY LEVEL: M

6.13. According to Skinner, biology is important because

a. it determines an organism's range of potential responses
b. it determines an organism's susceptibility to environmental influences
c. it determines an organism's actual behaviors
d. it determines an organism's range of potential responses and an organism's actual behaviors
e. it determines an organism's range of potential responses and an organism's susceptibility to specific environmental influences

ANSWER: E
DIFFICULTY LEVEL: C

6.14. Radical determinism states that

a. only a small amount of behavior is caused by the environment
b. approximately 50% of behavior is caused by the environment
c. the majority of behavior is caused by the environment
d. all behavior is caused by the environment
e. no behavior is caused by the environment

ANSWER: D
DIFFICULTY LEVEL: M

6.15. Although Hull believed in the importance of environmental reinforcements for learning, he

a. also believed that the internal state of the organism was important
b. chose not to study learning behavior
c. believed that environmental reinforcements were unimportant in determining what behaviors would actually be performed
d. felt it was morally wrong to use environmental reinforcements to shape behavior
e. none of the above

ANSWER: A
DIFFICULTY LEVEL: M

6.16. __________ are credited with the creation of social learning theory.

a. Watson & Skinner
b. Dollard & Miller
c. Watson & Dollard
d. Miller & Skinner
e. Dollard & Skinner

ANSWER: B
DIFFICULTY LEVEL: C

6.17. A "habit hierarchy" describes

a. a learned hierarchy of likelihoods that a person will respond to a situation in a specific way, based on predicted rewards
b. a hierarchy of rewards which are all possible outcomes of a behavior, and which vary along the dimension of desirability
c. a hierarchy of punishments which are all possible outcomes of a behavior, and which vary along the dimension of undesirability
d. a small number of habitual responses that an individual will display in the vast majority of situations, regardless of situational characteristics
e. none of the above

ANSWER: A
DIFFICULTY LEVEL: C

6.18. In his studies with Rhesus monkeys, Harlow found that
a. infant monkeys became attached to the mothers that gave them food
b. infant monkeys became attached to whatever mother they were given
c. infant monkeys became attached to the cloth mothers, regardless of whether these mothers provided food
d. infant monkeys became attached to the wire mothers, regardless of whether these mothers provided food
e. infant monkeys became attached to all objects in their cages

ANSWER: C
DIFFICULTY LEVEL: E

6.19. When a primary drive impels someone toward a behavior and a secondary drives impels the person away from that same behavior, _______ develops.
a. an approach-approach conflict
b. an approach-avoidance conflict
c. an avoidance-avoidance conflict
d. an avoidance-aggression conflict
e. an avoidance-frustration conflict

ANSWER: B
DIFFICULTY LEVEL: M

6.20. The frustration-aggression hypothesis is best illustrated by which of the following?
a. you are hungry and so you get something from the refrigerator to eat
b. you are hungry but you have planned a special dinner with your spouse and so you decide not to snack before dinner; instead you watch TV
c. you are hungry and you decide to eat some leftovers from last night; when you go to the kitchen you see that your sister left them out all night and that they are now moldy, so you yell at her
d. you are hungry but there is nothing good in the house to eat; you go to the store and purchase a frozen dinner and some soda
e. none of the above illustrate the frustration-aggression hypothesis

ANSWER: C
DIFFICULTY LEVEL: M

6.21. Sears described personality as "potentialities for action" which included
- a. motivation
- b. expectations
- c. habit structure
- d. environmental events produced by a behavior
- e. all of the above

ANSWER: E
DIFFICULTY LEVEL: M

6.22. The studies of child-rearing precursors of dependency and aggression in children (as studied by Sears) showed that
- a. child-rearing practices were completely unrelated to personality characteristics
- b. parents' reports of how much they punished the child were related to the child's dependency and aggression
- c. parents' reports of how much they punished the child were related to the child's dependency but not aggression
- d. parents' reports of how much they punished the child were related to the child's aggression but not dependency
- e. child-rearing practices were found to be highly related to all personality outcomes examined, not just in the areas of dependency and aggression

ANSWER: B
DIFFICULTY LEVEL: C

6.23. The quote that behaviorism "has substituted for the erstwhile anthropomorphic view of the rat, a ratomorphic view of man" implies that
- a. rats and humans are the same in terms of how they learn
- b. behaviorism replaces our humanness with simple laws derived from rat studies
- c. it is better to study rats than humans because there are fewer ethical issues involved
- d. we should not try to draw comparisons between humans and rats
- e. a behavioristic view of personality is completely without merit

ANSWER: B
DIFFICULTY LEVEL: E

6.24. Social cognitive learning theories differ from Dollard & Miller's social learning theory in which of the following ways?
a. they emphasize the importance of the social context in personality
b. they reject the idea that environments are important contributors to personality
c. they assume that personality is impossible to study because it is internal, but posit that learning can be studied
d. all of the above
e. none of the above

ANSWER: A
DIFFICULTY LEVEL: M

6.25. Which of the following types of reinforcement is described as important by social cognitive learning theorists?
a. self-reinforcement
b. vicarious reinforcement
c. social reinforcement
d. all of the above
e. none of the above

ANSWER: D
DIFFICULTY LEVEL: M

6.26. Harlow's famous studies of Rhesus monkeys in which infant monkeys were separated from their mothers was designed to test the notion of:
a. self-reinforcement
b. primary drives
c. secondary drives
d. tertiary drives
e. the drives of "big bertha"

ANSWER: C
DIFFICULTY LEVEL: M

6.27. Dollard and Miller's learning theory explains neurotic behavior in terms of:
a. self-reinforcement (masturbation)
b. primary drives being repressed
c. approach-avoidance conflicts
d. tertiary drives and classical conditioning
e. the example of "big bertha"

ANSWER: C
DIFFICULTY LEVEL: M

6.28. When Jennifer first came home from the hospital as a baby she had colic and often cried. Her parents were terribly worried about her and became distressed whenever she would begin to sob. Although Jennifer is now nearly four, and the colic has long since disappeared, her parents both experience a sense of restlessness and anxiety whenever they hear a baby crying. In this situation, anxiety is a
a. unconditioned stimulus
b. conditioned response
c. condemnation response
d. conditioned stimulus
e. intergenerational stimulus

ANSWER: B
DIFFICULTY LEVEL: M

6.29. If you suffered from arachnophobia (extreme fear of spiders) you might seek the help of a therapist in overcoming your problem. Which of the following would be a legitimate but somewhat risky method of treatment?
a. systematizing
b. sensitizing
c. trans-sensitizing
d. flooding
e. hurricaning

ANSWER: D
DIFFICULTY LEVEL: M

6.30. Superstitious behaviors, such as wearing a lucky ring or eating special foods prior to an important event are best explained by
- a. operant conditioning
- b. classical conditioning
- c. primary conditioning
- d. secondary conditioning
- e. tertiary conditioning

ANSWER: A
DIFFICULTY LEVEL: M

2.10 F

6.31. According to Skinner, the motivations that Freud called the drives of the id are better understood as:
- a. biological reinforcers of the environment
- b. the internalization of punishment
- c. the classical conditioning of intrinsic motivation
- d. the remote controls of the Skinner box
- e. the reinforcments of old age

ANSWER: A
DIFFICULTY LEVEL: M

6.32. Great-uncle Lyle seems to have lost all motivation to be active. He finds it hard to get to work and to enjoy recreation. He often says that things "just aren't worth doing." Skinner would suggest that this behavior pattern is a result of:
- a. Evolutionarily selected aging processes
- b. Classically conditioned apathy
- c. Negative reinforcement
- d. Low self-esteem
- e. A lack of behavioral reinforcements

ANSWER: E
DIFFICULTY LEVEL: M

6.33. According to Skinner, to maximize one's potential,one should:
   a. Arrange his/her environment to facilitate maximal behavior
   b. Seek appropriate reinforcers of desired behavior
   c. Administer punishments to those responsible for limiting his/her potential
   d. Get in touch with his/her punished inner child
   e. Both a and b

   ANSWER: E
   DIFFICULTY LEVEL: M

6.34. Skinner asserts that feelings...
   a. Are sometimes important in causing behavior
   b. Help us understand the science of behavior
   c. Are collateral products of our genetic and environmental histories
   d. Are collateral products of learned identity formations
   e. Both a and b

   ANSWER: C
   DIFFICULTY LEVEL: M

6.35. According to Skinner, part of the reason that the science of behavior has not progressed as far as it should is due to:
   a. Our experience with and interest in our own feelings and states of mind as being causally related to behavior
   b. Our inclination to look at internal processes of others as causing behavior
   c. The attitude that searching for the causes of human behavior in the environment is an attack on humankind's dignity
   d. The attitude that searching for the causes of human behavior in the environment is an attack on humankind's freedom
   e. All of the above

   ANSWER: E
   DIFFICULTY LEVEL: M

6.36. It is said that there is no price for good health—life is priceless. Yet if hospitals are paid for costs associated with all Medicare patient costs, the bills skyrocket. If hospitals receive a fixed amount of money for each Medicare patient they treat, the numbers of patients go up but the length of stay decreases. If doctors receive a fixed amount of money per patient in their group, then hospitalization rates go down. This phenomenon is most easily explained by which basic approach to understanding individual human behavior?
a. psychoanalytic
b. neo-analytic
c. biological
d. behaviorist
e. statistical

ANSWER: D
DIFFICULTY LEVEL: M

6.37. Skinner asserts that to address social and cultural problems, we should:
a. Convince people of their free will, emphasizing the consequent ability to choose to behave in more socially constructive ways
b. Manipulate the environment, which really controls behavior
c. Appeal more reliably to people's feelings of community
d. Actually, there is little hope of improving society, thus his book "Beyond Freedom and Dignity"
e. Increase funding for social research

ANSWER: B
DIFFICULTY LEVEL: E

6.38. How does extinction of a response occur?
a. the conditioned stimulus is no longer paired with the unconditioned stimulus
b. once a response is conditioned, it cannot be extinguished
c. the reinforcement rate is increased
d. reinforcement is shifted to a variable-interval schedule
e. none of the above

ANSWER: A
DIFFICULTY LEVEL: M

6.39. A client comes to a therapist complaining of a great fear (phobia) of heights. The therapist first has the individual describe and think about increasingly high places. Next he goes with the client to the first floor of a building, all the while encouraging and reassuring. They spend time looking out the window until the client is comfortable, then they go up one floor. Gradually they work their way up to the top floor of a very high skyscraper. The treatment method the therapist is employing is called:
a. deconditioning
b. flooding
c. systematic desensitization
d. unconditioning
e. reconditioning

ANSWER: C
DIFFICULTY LEVEL: M

6.40. Skinner's approach would suggest that many problems faced by old people are due in large part to:
a. long ago established but maladaptive learned behaviors
b. shortcomings in the environment
c. discrimination against older individuals
d. anxiety in the face of mortality
e. Both a and b

ANSWER: E
DIFFICULTY LEVEL: M

6.41. Of the following reinforcement schedules, which is most effective in terms of creating a behavior that is resistant to extinction?
a. continuous reinforcement
b. partial reinforcement
c. systematic desensitization
d. operant punishment
e. none of the above

ANSWER: B
DIFFICULTY LEVEL: C

Essay Questions

6.1. Briefly describe Pavlov's conditioning of neurotic behavior in dogs. What kind of insight does this give us into the way that neuroticism might be "conditioned" in humans?

6.2. What can be done to "extinguish" classically conditioned fear responses? Which method seems to work best? Why is it that classically conditioned fear responses are unlikely to be extinguished without some sort of intervention?

6.3. What is the difference between a positive and a negative reinforcer? How is a negative reinforcer different from a punishment?

6.4. Describe the basic tenets behind Skinner's book, Beyond Freedom and Dignity. Do you believe it would be possible to create a society like this? Do you think it would be a good idea? Why?

6.5. What is the difference between a primary drive and a secondary drive? According to Dollard & Miller, how are drives related to "habits"?

6.6. How does the concept of reinforcement help to explain varying normative levels of personality "traits" in different cultures?

6.7. How did Dollard & Miller reconcile their theories with the Freudian school of thought?

CHAPTER 7: COGNITIVE ASPECTS

Multiple Choice Questions

7.1. Which of the following is NOT one of the central tenets of Gestalt psychology?
  a. we seek meaning in our environments
  b. when presented with information we strive to ignore things that we have not experienced before
  c. we organize sensations from our environments into meaning-laden perceptions
  d. complex stimuli are more than just the sum of their parts
  e. none of the above

ANSWER: B
DIFFICULTY LEVEL: C

7.2. Lewin's "field theory" focused on the separateness vs. overlapping nature of aspects of a person's life, which he called ____________.
  a. life space
  b. death space
  c. time continuum
  d. atmosphere
  e. generation

ANSWER: A
DIFFICULTY LEVEL: M

7.3. Julie is a successful interior decorator. She says that her success is due to her ability to envision the "big picture" and to create beautiful rooms without becoming too focused on small particulars within the room. For instance, she can accurately place shelving above the fireplace, despite the fact that the fireplace bricks are crooked and sloping. She is most likely
  a. field dependent
  b. field independent
  c. field positional
  d. field dispositional
  e. positional dependent

ANSWER: B
DIFFICULTY LEVEL: M

7.4. In the rod-and-frame task, people that align the bar with the frame rather than making it vertical are ___________ and would probably ___________ in the body-positioning task.

a. field dependent; remain upright despite tilted room
b. field independent; tilt to align with the room
c. field independent; remain upright despite tilted room
d. field dependent; tilt to align with the room
e. field independent; be unable to position self in tilted room

ANSWER: D
DIFFICULTY LEVEL: M

7.5. A field dependent person is more sensitive to ___________ than a field independent person.

a. context of a problem
b. the "big picture"
c. social and interpersonal cues
d. all of the above
e. none of the above

ANSWER: D
DIFFICULTY LEVEL: M

7.6. Field dependency was first conceived as a personality variable by

a. Montgomery & Adler
b. Freud & Gambone
c. Witkin & Asch
d. Horney & Freud
e. James & Cohen

ANSWER: C
DIFFICULTY LEVEL: M

7.7. A person's placement on the field-dependence continuum has NOT been associated with

a. level of eye contact
b. career choices
c. socialization patterns
d. children's play preferences
e. career success

ANSWER: E
DIFFICULTY LEVEL: M

7.8. In general (at the group level),

a. females are somewhat more field dependent than males
b. males are somewhat more field dependent than females
c. females are more field dependent than males only in childhood
d. males are more field dependent than females only in childhood
e. none of the above

ANSWER: A
DIFFICULTY LEVEL: M

7.9. Schemas

a. are bundles of information that guide us and help us understand the world
b. are the specific situations we find ourselves in
c. are things that some people never develop
d. are never changed or modified after being formed
e. are independent of cultural environments

ANSWER: A
DIFFICULTY LEVEL: M

7.10. Our abilities to categorize stimuli are severely challenged when

a. we enter new houses
b. we encounter objects not even remotely similar to what we've experienced before
c. we buy new furniture
d. we meet new people
e. we move only in redundant environments which we have encountered many times

ANSWER: B
DIFFICULTY LEVEL: M

7.11. Stereotypes and prejudice are examples of the useful process of _______ becoming harmful.
   a. sublimation
   b. optimization
   c. contemporaneous judgment
   d. categorization
   e. perception

   ANSWER: D
   DIFFICULTY LEVEL: M

7.12. A confirmation bias is
   a. a tendency to say "yes" to requests that we don't really want to fulfill
   b. a preferential attending to information that confirms our expectations
   c. a bias in which we prefer to spend time with positive others
   d. all of the above
   e. none of the above

   ANSWER: B
   DIFFICULTY LEVEL: M

7.13. How we allocate our attention is a function of
   a. our current goals
   b. a few salient environmental features
   c. a combination of current goals and a few salient environmental features
   d. a variety of processes, none of which has been examined by researchers
   e. none of the above

   ANSWER: C
   DIFFICULTY LEVEL: M

7.14. Individuals with attention deficit disorder (ADD)
   a. are often able to concentrate intensely on a task that interests them
   b. often fail to shift their attention appropriately from task to task
   c. may be less sensitive to social cues
   d. all of the above
   e. can trace their problems to trouble with addition

   ANSWER: D
   DIFFICULTY LEVEL: M

7.15. Kelly's personal construct theory posits that
a. people are "scientists" who try to make sense of their worlds
b. people work hard to actively create their own personalities
c. people work hard to create other "persons" that they can interact with
d. individuals are largely immune to influences of their environments
e. a specific set of traits are necessary to explain an individual's personality

ANSWER: A
DIFFICULTY LEVEL: M

7.16. The personality assessment which requires individuals to describe how two people in his/her life differ from a third, thus identifying an important personality construct is the
a. Q-sort Test
b. Minnesota Multiphasic Personality Inventory
c. California Psychological Inventory
d. Role Construct Repertory Test
e. Rorschach Inkblot Test

ANSWER: D
DIFFICULTY LEVEL: M

7.17. Gardner's theory of multiple intelligences states that everyone has at least _______ different intelligences.
a. 2
b. 4
c. 5
d. 7
e. 16

ANSWER: D
DIFFICULTY LEVEL: M

7.18. Which of the following is NOT one of Gardner's multiple intelligences?
a. logical-mathematical intelligence
b. emotional intelligence
c. language intelligence
d. bodily-kinesthetic intelligence
e. conscientious intelligence

ANSWER: E
DIFFICULTY LEVEL: M

7.19. Cantor & Kihlstrom's idea of "social intelligence" describes
a. individual variation in social and interpersonal skills
b. individual variation in traditionally-measured intelligence
c. individual variation in musical and artistic aptitude
d. all of the above
e. none of the above

ANSWER: A
DIFFICULTY LEVEL: E

7.20. Individuals with an optimistic explanatory style
a. always perceive everything as positive
b. often see neutral events as positive, and find the "silver lining" in bad situations
c. explain things optimistically to others even though they don't believe it themselves
d. tend to focus on the negative side so that they will be pleasantly surprised
e. look at things very objectively and don't allow personal feelings to influence them

ANSWER: B
DIFFICULTY LEVEL: M

7.21. A pessimistic explanatory style
a. has been linked to depression
b. tend to focus on the negative aspects of situations
c. tend to have lower expectations for the future, based on pessimistic explanations of the present
d. all of the above
e. none of the above

ANSWER: D
DIFFICULTY LEVEL: M

7.22. Joyce recently lost her young son, and the experience was devastating. She was comforted, however, by the fact that her son's organs helped four other children to live longer. She now volunteers with children at a local day-care center, which reminds her of her son, and she is thankful that she had six years of happiness with him. Joyce's explanatory style is
a. optimistic
b. pessimistic
c. dual
d. social-constructivist
e. none of the above

ANSWER: A
DIFFICULTY LEVEL: M

7.23. Evan loves life! He sky-dives, scuba-dives, rides a motorcycle, and rock-climbs. His motto is: "you only live once" and he tries to get the most out of life by doing what he wants, eating what he wants (he was voted "junk-food-junkie" in high school), and throwing caution to the wind. When questioned about this, Evan declares that he is "lucky" and that he sincerely doubts that anything negative will happen to him. Evan's explanatory style is
a. optimistic
b. pessimistic
c. dual
d. social-constructivist
e. none of the above

ANSWER: A
DIFFICULTY LEVEL: M

7.24. Jena is a bright student, but she can't see it. Last week she got a B on her history test and was depressed for the rest of the afternoon. Her friends tried to cheer her up by offering to study with her next time, and reminding her that she'd done better than any of them, but it didn't help. In fact, Jena isn't just insecure about her scholastic abilities, but she also thinks she's ugly, fat, and without talent (the reality is that her looks are average, her weight is average, and she's a talented saxophone player). Jena's explanatory style is

a. optimistic
b. pessimistic
c. dual
d. social-constructivist
e. none of the above

ANSWER: B
DIFFICULTY LEVEL: M

7.25. Bandura's self-system is

a. the way a person perceives, evaluates, & regulates his/her own behavior so that it is appropriate and so that goals are achieved
b. a person's evaluation of him/herself which occurs at adolescence and once again at the transition to old age
c. a measurement tool which allows a therapist to determine what an individual thinks of him/herself, and which allows the client to be an active participant in any diagnosis
d. all of the above
e. none of the above

ANSWER: A
DIFFICULTY LEVEL: M

7.26. Observational learning is similar to the same as

a. vicarious learning
b. modeling
c. learning by watching others
d. all of the above
e. none of the above

ANSWER: D
DIFFICULTY LEVEL: C

7.27. Which of the following is true of Bandura's "Bobo doll" studies?
a. children who saw aggressive behavior by adults were less aggressive themselves
b. children who saw neutral behavior by adults were more aggressive themselves
c. children who saw aggressive behavior by adults were more aggressive themselves
d. children who saw aggressive behavior that was punished were more aggressive
e. children who saw neutral behavior that was punished were less aggressive

ANSWER: C
DIFFICULTY LEVEL: M

7.28. Which of the following influence whether or not a model's behavior will be repeated by an observer?
a. outcome expectancies
b. model's similarity to the observer
c. desirability of the behavior itself
d. all of the above
e. none of the above

ANSWER: D
DIFFICULTY LEVEL: C

7.29. The cognitive components that Bandura describes as necessary for the performance of modeled behavior are:
a. attention, retention, motor reproduction, and motivation
b. attention, desire, focus, and reproduction
c. attention, retention, detention, and motivation
d. attention, suspension, retention, and motor reproduction
e. attention, desire, retention, motor reproduction

ANSWER: A
DIFFICULTY LEVEL: C

7.30. Self-efficacy is
a. self-esteem
b. a belief about how competent one is to perform a behavior
c. explanatory style
d. all of the above
e. none of the above

ANSWER: B
DIFFICULTY LEVEL: M

7.31. Which of the following is the most important in influencing self-efficacy?
a. past successes and failures
b. vicarious experiences
c. verbal persuasion
d. emotional reaction
e. none of the above

ANSWER: A
DIFFICULTY LEVEL: M

7.32. According to Rotter, which of the following affect behavior?
a. outcome expectancies
b. reinforcement values
c. explanatory style
d. both outcome expectancies and reinforcement values
e. both reinforcement values and explanatory style

ANSWER: D
DIFFICULTY LEVEL: C

7.33. When do we tend to weigh generalized expectancies most heavily?
a. in novel situations
b. in familiar situations
c. in situations with lots of people
d. in one-on-one situations
e. none of the above

ANSWER: A
DIFFICULTY LEVEL: C

7.34. Which of the following is NOT one of Rotter's six psychological needs?
a. recognition-status
b. independence
c. openness
d. love and affection
e. physical comfort

ANSWER: C
DIFFICULTY LEVEL: C

7.35. Rotter initially described the dimensions of locus-of-control (LOC) as __________, but more recently LOC has been found to be comprised of __________.

a. internality/externality; luck/powerful others/internality
b. internality/externality; luck/self/stability
c. powerful others/internality; internality/externality/luck
d. internality/luck; powerful others/externality/self
e. none of the above

ANSWER: A
DIFFICULTY LEVEL: M

7.36. Individuals with an internal LOC are more likely to be

a. achievement oriented
b. high achievers
c. low achievers
d. achievement oriented and high achievers
e. achievement oriented and low achievers

ANSWER: D
DIFFICULTY LEVEL: C

7.37. Learned helplessness describes a situation in which

a. individuals do not try to move around on their own
b. individuals believe that they are not in control of what happens to them
c. individuals are more attuned to the needs of others than they previously were
d. individuals believe that they can make important changes in their lives
e. individuals talk excessively about change, but do not actually change anything

ANSWER: B
DIFFICULTY LEVEL: M

7.38. Under a cognitive approach, thought processes are viewed as:

a. a cause of behavior
b. a consequence of behavior
c. a correlate of behavior
d. all of the above
e. none of the above

ANSWER: D
DIFFICULTY LEVEL: M

7.39. Bandura's view of modeling is that it:
   a. Is an efficient and prevalent way of transmitting and modifying behavior
   b. Is the primary way that cultural behavioral repertoires are acquired
   c. Can result in new behaviors in an individual
   d. Can strengthen or inhibit responses in an individual
   e. All of the above

   ANSWER: E
   DIFFICULTY LEVEL: C

7.40. Bandura states that in traditional behaviorism, it is believed that for learning to occur:
   a. The subject must execute the behavior
   b. The response must be reinforced or punished during learning
   c. Only models that are valued by the subject are effective
   d. The important factors of memory and attention must be properly utilized
   e. Both a and b

   ANSWER: E
   DIFFICULTY LEVEL: C

7.41. George Kelly states that the unique set of personal constructs that each person has:
   a. Is what makes each person a unique individual
   b. Is what determines an individual's view of reality
   c. Determines the direction of movement, the choices a person makes
   d. Is arranged in a network of interdependent constructs
   e. All of the above

   ANSWER: E
   DIFFICULTY LEVEL: M

7.42. When John meets new people, he immediately thinks about whether he has greater intellectual capacity than they do. George Kelly's theory would suggest that:

a. John's behavior is likely to change with the situation, so he won't always see people in these terms.
b. John has a construct for smart vs. dumb
c. John is overcompensating for low intellectual self-esteem
d. John has a construct for defensiveness against smart people
e. Both a and b

ANSWER: B
DIFFICULTY LEVEL: M

7.43. In George Kelly's theory, what guides a person's behavior?

a. The individual's standings on the Big 5 factors of personality
b. The reinforcement history of the individual which leads to habitual behavioral patterns and choices
c. The individual's answers to existential questions
d. The constructs an individual has and his/her expectations and interpretations of the environment
e. The individual's standing on need for achievement (n Ach)

ANSWER: D
DIFFICULTY LEVEL: E

Essay Questions

7.1. Describe field dependence vs. field independence. Is this a dichotomous or a continuous construct? In what types of situations would greater field dependence be an asset? When would field independence be most desirable?

7.2. What is the difference between a schema and a script?

7.3. In general, an optimistic explanatory style seems most adaptive. Why is this? Can someone be too optimistic?

7.4. If you had a friend who did not believe in his/her abilities to succeed in his/her job, what would you do to increase his/her self-efficacy? Why would you choose this method?

7.5. Briefly describe how "vicarious learning" occurs. What are some of the things that determine whether or not a learned behavior is actually performed?

7.6. How might the concept of vicarious or observational learning be reconciled with a behaviorist approach to learning?

7.7. Why might an observational learning approach be superior to a behavioral learning approach when acquiring skills such as driving or tightrope walking?

7.8. Based on what was discovered in Bandura's "Bobo doll" studies, how might we learn to inhibit behaviors that are socially inappropriate without actually doing them and being punished?

7.9. Why, with all our technologies, are we still unable to create a computer that accurately simulates a human?

CHAPTER 8 : TRAIT AND SKILL ASPECTS

Multiple Choice Questions

8.1. People have been using traits to describe others for:

a. approximately a decade
b. more than a century
c. thousands of years
d. only the past five years
e. approximately three decades

ANSWER: C
DIFFICULTY LEVEL: E

8.2. According to Hippocrates, those with choleric humors were:

a. hopeful and cheerful
b. angry and irascible
c. depressive and sad
d. apathetic and dull
e. depressive and happy

ANSWER: B
DIFFICULTY LEVEL: M

8.3. Carl Jung's definition of extraversion included:

a. a focus on things outside the self
b. loud and boisterous expressions
c. deep thinking and introspection
d. all of the above
e. none of the above

ANSWER: A
DIFFICULTY LEVEL: M

8.4. A personality measure based on Jung's introversion and extraversion is the:
a. Minnesota Multiphasic Personality Inventory
b. California Psychological Inventory
c. California Critical Thinking Inventory
d. NEO Personality Inventory
e. Myers Briggs Type Indicator

ANSWER: E
DIFFICULTY LEVEL: M

8.5. The Big Five refers to:
a. five broadly defined personality traits
b. the five indicators of Neuroticism
c. the founders of modern personality theory
d. the most-used questionnaires in personality assessment
e. none of the above

ANSWER: A
DIFFICULTY LEVEL: E

8.6. Cattell used _____ to organize adjectives into trait-categories.
a. regression
b. ANOVA
c. factor analysis
d. T-tests
e. LISREL

ANSWER: C
DIFFICULTY LEVEL: M

8.7. Q-data and L-data refer to:
a. Quail-data and Lizard-data
b. Qualitative-data and Life-data
c. Questionnaire-data and Likelihood-data
d. Questionnaire-data and Life-data
e. Quantitative-data and Likelihood-data

ANSWER: D
DIFFICULTY LEVEL: C

8.8. Cattell named his 16 personality factors with letters of the alphabet because:
- a. he didn't want people to be biased by the names
- b. it was important for them to be alphabetical
- c. it was suggested by a colleague
- d. letters fit better into mathematical equations
- e. both b and d were important considerations

ANSWER: A
DIFFICULTY LEVEL: E

8.9. A trait approach to personality is very
- a. situation centered
- b. person centered
- c. both a and b
- d. all of the above
- e. none of the above

ANSWER: B
DIFFICULTY LEVEL: M

8.10. Allport was concerned with issues of: Other than his work of traits, Allport was
- a. prejudice
- b. ~~cultural~~ beh'l influences on personality
- c. schizophrenia ~~in a religious context~~
- d. all of the above
- e. ~~a and b only~~ none of the above

ANSWER: E
DIFFICULTY LEVEL: C

8.11. The behaviorist work of Skinner particularly bothered:
- a. Jung
- b. Cattell
- c. Allport
- d. Spearman
- e. Brown

ANSWER: C
DIFFICULTY LEVEL: C

8.12. Allport's "common traits" are:
a. traits that many people share
b. traits which are least theoretically interesting
c. traits uncovered by factor analytic techniques
d. traits that are difficult to define
e. traits which are boring

ANSWER: A
DIFFICULTY LEVEL: M

8.13. According to _____, it would be important to understand the origins of motivations or strivings.
a. Allport
b. Skinner
c. Darwin
d. Freud
e. Pavlov

ANSWER: D
DIFFICULTY LEVEL: C

8.14. The term "proprium" refers to:
a. a person's outward behavior
b. the inner core of someone's personality
c. counterintuitive behaviors
d. all of the above
e. none of the above

ANSWER: B
DIFFICULTY LEVEL: E

8.15. Personal dispositions that greatly influence behavior are termed:
a. cardinal dispositions
b. incarnate dispositions
c. superordinate dispositions
d. motivational dispositions
e. transcendental dispositions

ANSWER: A
DIFFICULTY LEVEL: E

F

8.16. Which of the following is NOT one of the Big Five?
a. Neuroticism
b. Extraversion
c. Openness
d. Agreeableness
e. Eclecticism

ANSWER: E
DIFFICULTY LEVEL: C

8.17. How might we determine whether or not the "Big Five" really exist?
a. by finding their biological counterparts
b. by finding them in other cultures
c. by showing that they accurately predict behavior
d. all of the above may help to demonstrate their reality
e. none of the above will enlighten us as to their reality

ANSWER: D
DIFFICULTY LEVEL: C

8.18. Of the following, which make up Eysenck's "big three"?
a. Neuroticism, Extraversion, & Openness
b. Neuroticism, Extraversion, & Psychoticism
c. Neuroticism, Psychoticism, & Ego Control
d. Extraversion, Openness, & Psychoticism
e. Neuroticism, Extraversion, & Ego Control

ANSWER: B
DIFFICULTY LEVEL: E

8.19. If five people agree that Carol is extraverted, this means:
a. she really is extraverted
b. the five people share the same biases in their ratings
c. either a or b could be true
d. neither a nor b could be true
e. the scale is highly valid

ANSWER: C
DIFFICULTY LEVEL: C

8.20. In general, the easiest traits to recognize in others are:
a. Extraversion and Conscientiousness
b. Neuroticism and Conscientiousness
c. Openness and Agreeableness
d. Openness and Neuroticism
e. Neuroticism and Extraversion

ANSWER: A
DIFFICULTY LEVEL: M

8.21. The founder of a motive-based study of personality was:
a. Murray
b. Allport
c. Eysenck
d. Cattell
e. Shipley

ANSWER: A
DIFFICULTY LEVEL: C

8.22. According to Murray, a person's "Basic Needs" include:
a. Need for Affiliation
b. Need for Exhibition
c. Need for Achievement
d. all of the above
e. none of the above

ANSWER: D
DIFFICULTY LEVEL: C

8.23. Charismatic people often tend to be:
a. hostile
b. emotionally expressive
c. emotionally unexpressive
d. aloof
e. none of the above

ANSWER: B
DIFFICULTY LEVEL: E

8.24. Expressive people are often perceived as:
- a. attractive
- b. personable
- c. negligent
- d. both a and b
- e. both b and c

ANSWER: D
DIFFICULTY LEVEL: M

8.25. Dominant people tend to:
- a. speak more loudly
- b. move more expansively
- c. control eye contact (stare or look away, as they like)
- d. all of the above
- e. none of the above

ANSWER: D
DIFFICULTY LEVEL: M

8.26. In a situation where an *expressive* person is trying to hide his or her emotions and an *unexpressive* person is acting naturally:
- a. generally, they act about the same
- b. generally, the unexpressive person now shows more emotion
- c. generally, the expressive person still shows more emotion
- d. now neither one shows any emotion
- e. this type of study has never been done

ANSWER: C
DIFFICULTY LEVEL: M

8.27. Having good ______ has been called "personal intelligence."
- a. emotional and nonverbal abilities
- b. knowledge about the self
- c. knowledge about personality psychology
- d. none of the above
- e. all of the above

ANSWER: A
DIFFICULTY LEVEL: E

8.28. Eysenck would combine Cattell's factors of outgoingness and assertiveness and call this:

a. Agreeableness
b. Extraversion
c. Openness
d. Conscientiousness
e. Neuroticism

ANSWER: B
DIFFICULTY LEVEL: E

8.29. Peer-ratings of personality tend to be:

a. identical to self-ratings
b. the same as stranger-ratings
c. more accurate than stranger-ratings
d. very unreliable
e. none of the above

ANSWER: C
DIFFICULTY LEVEL: M

8.30. The idea of "social" or "emotional" intelligence combines:

a. nonverbal social skills and nontraditional intelligence
b. nonverbal social skills and mathematical skills
c. emotional or social propensity and IQ
d. all of the above
e. none of the above

ANSWER: A
DIFFICULTY LEVEL: E

8.31. If you are interested in defining, as simply as possible, what makes a "good friend," you might list all of the things you value in a friend, and then use a statistical procedure based on correlations to narrow all of these down into just a few basic categories or dimensions. This type of analysis is called

a. factor analysis
b. multiple regression analysis
c. item response analysis
d. multi-directional analysis
e. temporal analysis

ANSWER: A
DIFFICULTY LEVEL: M

8.32. Which of the following traits is most difficult to measure?

a. agreeableness
b. extraversion
c. neuroticism
d. openness
e. conscientiousness

ANSWER: D
DIFFICULTY LEVEL: C

8.33. Becky is an excellent figure-skater—in fact she may be eligible for the next Olympic Games. Becky is certainly high in ______________ intelligence.

a. linguistic gliding
b. bodily-kinesthetic
c. logical-mathematical
d. spatio-orbital
e. athletic-sports

ANSWER: B
DIFFICULTY LEVEL: E

8.34. "Heidi is aggressive and extroverted." This statement describes Heidi in terms of:
a. types
b. traits
d. drives
c. motives
e. cannot be determined due to unreliability

ANSWER: B
DIFFICULTY LEVEL: E

8.35. Gordon Allport's definition of personality states that personality is "A dynamic organization." By this he means:
a. A unique network or organization of personal constructs characterizes every one of us, making us all dynamic creatures
b. There is an organization of mental structures and processes that is constantly changing
c. Dynamic theories such as Freud's psychoanalytic theory are essentially correct but should include more emphasis on the true organization of personality
d. The organization of personality traits interact with environmental presses in a dynamic, fluid manner to determine an individual's behavior
e. Both a and b

ANSWER: D
DIFFICULTY LEVEL: M

8.36. Which is NOT a characteristic of traits as defined by Allport?
a. They are biophysical facts
b. They are inferred from observations of behavior
c. They are constructions created by the cognitive processing of observers
d. Traits and other processes determine behavior
e. All (the above) are characteristics

ANSWER: E
DIFFICULTY LEVEL: M

8.37. Which concept would Allport be most likely to address with his approach to the study of personality?

a. Unconscious forces guiding behavior
b. Social learning forces guiding behavior
c. Chumship and mental health
d. Free will and self actualization
e. Cross-situational consistency of behavior

ANSWER: E
DIFFICULTY LEVEL: C

8.38. Which of the following criticisms of the trait approach to personality is(are) addressed by Allport's work?

a. Trait psychology ignores unconscious forces, which is where the action in personality really is
b. The genetic basis of specific traits is not known
c. People's behavior varies from situation to situation, so speaking of consistent traits that cause behavior is groundless
d. Both a and b
e. Both b and c

ANSWER: C
DIFFICULTY LEVEL: C

8.39. According to R. McCrae and O. John, the Big 5 factors of personality are:

a. Extraversion, neuroticism, openness, self-actualization, and eclecticism
b. Self-actualization, valuing, congruence, ability to love, and assertiveness
c. Extraversion, neuroticism, openness, conscientiousness, and agreeableness
d. constructedness, cognition, situational variability, neuroticism, and extroversion
e. None of the above

ANSWER: C
DIFFICULTY LEVEL: C

8.40. Which factor in the Five Factor Model is the source of most controversy?

a. Neuroticism
b. Self-actualization
c. Openness
d. Situational variability
e. Eclecticism

ANSWER: C
DIFFICULTY LEVEL: M

8.41. Significant criticism of the Five Factor Model is that:

a. Five is too few factors to describe personality
b. Five is more factors than is needed to describe personality
c. The Big 5 are not real personality traits, but merely reflect people's social reputations
d. The Big 5 are simply a function of observer's cognitive biases
e. All of these are significant criticisms

ANSWER: A
DIFFICULTY LEVEL: C

8.42. One characteristic that differentiates Eysenck's conceptualization of the major traits from the Big Five approach is that Eysenck attempts to take into account

a. Freudian theory
b. underlying biological influences
c. Causal Modeling statistical techniques
d. Jungian archetypes
e. None of the above

ANSWER: B
DIFFICULTY LEVEL: M

8.43. Which is NOT a positive (useful) aspect of the Five Factor Model of personality?

a. It provides a common language for psychologists to use to communicate about personality
b. It is a basic phenomenon to be explained
c. It provides a framework for organizing research
d. It provides most everything you need to know about personality
e. It provides a guide to personality assessment

ANSWER: B
DIFFICULTY LEVEL: C

Essay Questions

8.1. Briefly describe what happened to Allport when he, at the age of 22, visited Freud for the first time. What did this incident teach him?

8.2. Why might the idea that every person has an entirely unique personality be problematic for some psychologists?

8.3. Choose one of the Big Five dimensions of personality and write a short character sketch of someone high on this trait. Be specific, using a real person you know (you do not need to identify the person).

8.4. Why are some personality traits easier to recognize and rate than others?

8.5. What are motives and how are motives different from traits?

8.6. Do you prefer Cattell's 16-factor approach to personality, or Eysenck's 3-factor approach? Why?

Final

8.7. Trent is a high school student who is often getting into trouble. His teachers say that he is constantly talking in class, has too much energy to stay in his seat, and passes notes to classmates. Although he often fails to turn in assignments and thus has poor grades, his instructors agree that he is creative and bright--his jokes are witty, and on occasion he asks surprisingly perceptive questions. Because of his classroom behavior, Trent is not a favorite with teachers, but his classmates all like him, saying that he is friendly, fun to be around, and kind. Trent, himself, says that he is content with the way his life is and that he wouldn't change a thing. He is not worried about the future, and believes that in the long run his winning personality will enable him to accomplish his goals.

Based on the description you have just read, rate Trent as either high, average, or low on each of the Big Five dimensions of personality, and then justify your ratings.

8.8. June is six years old and her parents are worried about her. She spends a lot of time in her room and doesn't seem to enjoy being with other children. In addition, she seems to spend a lot of time worrying about things that most children don't think of, such as what might happen if there were a nuclear war, whether her house might burn down, or if someone might kidnap her. Her mother reports that she is a very "good" child who keeps her room clean and always remembers to feed her puppy. Both of her parents also agree that she is eager to please others, and her father notes that the tendency of the neighbor children to argue and fight might be contributing to her reluctance to play with them--June hates arguing. This little girl loves to paint and draw, and her parents believe her to be quite talented. She also has a vocabulary that is larger than that of most children her age, and a very active imagination. As long as she is not forced to interact with other children, she seems reasonably happy.

Based on the description you have just read, rate June as either high, average, or low on each of the Big Five dimensions of personality, and then justify your ratings.

CHAPTER 9: HUMANISTIC AND EXISTENTIAL ASPECTS

Multiple Choice Questions

9.1. In basic terms, existentialism is ________.

a. an area of philosophy concerned with death and dying
b. an area of philosophy concerned with interpersonal relationships
c. an area of philosophy concerned with the meaning of human existence
d. an area of philosophy concerned with entrances to other worlds
e. an area of philosophy concerned with how we choose religions

ANSWER: C
DIFFICULTY LEVEL: E

9.2. Positivists advocate _______ while non-positivists argue ________.

a. the governing laws of behavior; the subjective nature of existence
b. the subjective nature of existence; for the governing laws of behavior
c. that there is no existence; that existence must be operationally defined
d. positive thinking as a way to happiness; that we must be realistic in judging ourselves
e. none of the above

ANSWER: A
DIFFICULTY LEVEL: M

9.3. A phenomenological approach to personality states that

a. we are the products of the phenomena that we encounter
b. people's perceptions and subjective realities are important and should be studied
c. phenomena that occur in childhood are more important than what occurs later
d. only objective events, and not perceptions, are valid when studying personality
e. people vary in the degree to which they create their own phenomena

ANSWER: B
DIFFICULTY LEVEL: M

9.4. Maslow stated that psychoanalysis and behaviorism were the first two "forces" and that ________ was the "third force."
  a. love
  b. neo-analysis
  c. existentialism
  d. extroversion
  e. humanism

ANSWER: E
DIFFICULTY LEVEL: M

210 F 9.5. Humanism emphasizes
  a. the personal worth of the individual
  b. the importance of human values
  c. the creative, active, spontaneous nature of humanity
  d. that we strive to achieve fulfillment and to create our futures
  e. all of the above

ANSWER: E
DIFFICULTY LEVEL: C

9.6. The dialogue in which each person confirms the other as being unique and important is called
  a. the "I-It" dialogue
  b. the "I-Me-Me-Mine" dialogue
  c. the "I-Thou" dialogue
  d. the "You-Us" dialogue
  e. the "Us-Them" dialogue

ANSWER: C
DIFFICULTY LEVEL: M

9.7. The purpose of many of the encounter groups, hippie communes, and meditation seminars in the 1960s and 1970s was to
   a. serve as a cover for the illegal drug-culture
   b. help people realize their inner potentials
   c. help people recover from the traumatic experiences of war
   d. discourage people from being independent
   e. create new and uniform identities for people so that they could function like robots

   ANSWER: B
   DIFFICULTY LEVEL: M

9.8. Fromm would argue that
   a. love is something that most of us simply stumble into
   b. love is something that is difficult to understand and probably has little meaning
   c. the capacity to love is not something we develop, but something we are born with
   d. love requires knowledge, effort, and experience
   e. none of the above

   ANSWER: D
   DIFFICULTY LEVEL: M

9.9. According to Fromm, the most mature and healthy personality is one that
   a. has learned to ignore the environment
   b. transcends everyday life and is productive, respectful, and loving of others
   c. has experienced virtually all that life has to offer, so that there are no surprises
   d. all of the above
   e. none of the above

   ANSWER: B
   DIFFICULTY LEVEL: C

9.10. Which of the following provides some evidence that Fromm's ideas might be right?
  a. in Western countries, psychological depression has been steadily rising for the past 50 years
  b. in Western countries, psychological depression has been steadily decreasing for the past 50 years
  c. communal societies have been found to have more violent crimes than non-communal societies
  d. divorce is on the decline in America
  e. none of the above

ANSWER: A
DIFFICULTY LEVEL: M

9.11. Rogers believed that
  a. people have an inherent tendency toward stagnation
  b. people have an inherent tendency toward violence
  c. people have an inherent tendency toward growth
  d. people have an inherent tendency for isolation
  e. people have an inherent tendency for substance-abuse

ANSWER: C
DIFFICULTY LEVEL: C

9.12. Many humanistic psychologists have deep roots in
  a. biology
  b. mathematics
  c. history
  d. religion
  e. art

ANSWER: D
DIFFICULTY LEVEL: M

9.13. According to Rogers, a healthy person
a. has a broad self-concept and is open to many feelings and experiences
b. has a narrow and well-defined self-concept
c. is someone who has had a preponderance of positive experiences in life
d. a. and c.
e. none of the above

ANSWER: A
DIFFICULTY LEVEL: M

9.14. For therapy to be successful, Rogers argues that
a. the therapist must have unconditional positive regard for the client
b. the therapist must empathize with and understand the client fully
c. the therapist must communicate the client's internal frame-of-reference back to him/her
d. all of the above
e. none of the above

ANSWER: D
DIFFICULTY LEVEL: M

9.15. You are driving on the highway and a careless driver cuts you off, nearly causing a wreck. As if that were not enough, she then yells obscenities at you from her car and shakes her fist. Rogers would say that the most adaptive things for you to do would be to
a. let your anger out and yell something nasty back at her
b. immediately think happy thoughts and not allow any anger to cloud your mind
c. acknowledge your anger but not act aggressively, instead try to be understanding and compassionate
d. teach her an object-lesson by cutting her off and then yelling at her so she knows how it feels
e. none of the above

ANSWER: C
DIFFICULTY LEVEL: C

9.16. Rollo May sees _______ as being a fundamental aspect of human existence.
   a. anxiety
   b. pets
   c. socioeconomic status
   d. intelligence
   e. worldly possessions

   ANSWER: A
   DIFFICULTY LEVEL: M

9.17. Which of the following interventions to help people with life-threatening illnesses has its roots in existential-humanistic psychology?
   a. aversive conditioning therapy
   b. support groups
   c. psychotherapy
   d. antibiotic therapy
   e. systematic desensitization

   ANSWER: B
   DIFFICULTY LEVEL: M

9.18. According to your textbook, in the debate between Skinner and May, who was proved right?
   a. Skinner
   b. May
   c. they were both right
   d. neither one was correct
   e. the book did not discuss the outcome of the debate

   ANSWER: C
   DIFFICULTY LEVEL: M

9.19. Self-actualization, an important component of an existentialist/humanistic approach to personality was first proposed by
   a. Freud
   b. Adler
   c. Jung
   d. Horney
   e. Maslow

   ANSWER: C
   DIFFICULTY LEVEL: C

9.20. According to Maslow, self-actualized people
a. are independent
b. have a love of humankind
c. have strong ethical principles
d. all of the above
e. none of the above

ANSWER: D
DIFFICULTY LEVEL: M

9.21. Which of the following is NOT characteristic of a peak experience?
a. focus on the experience, activity, or event is intense
b. other things in the environment recede into the background
c. time seems to stand still
d. there is a heightened sense of anxiety
e. there is a sense of well-being

ANSWER: D
DIFFICULTY LEVEL: M

9.22. According to Maslow's hierarchy of needs, which must be satisfied first?
a. physiological needs
b. safety needs
c. belonging and love needs
d. esteem needs
e. Maslow only argues that all needs must be met, not that they must be met in a particular order

ANSWER: A
DIFFICULTY LEVEL: M

9.23. Maslow based his theories on the study of
a. schizophrenic patients
b. individuals with eating disorders
c. well-adjusted people
d. homeless individuals
e. lobotomized patients in mental institutions

ANSWER: C
DIFFICULTY LEVEL: M

9.24. The Personal Orientation Inventory was designed to assess
a. fish-like Hawaiian depression
b. self-actualization
c. self-efficacy
d. psychopathology
e. explanatory style

ANSWER: B
DIFFICULTY LEVEL: C

9.25. The existentialist/humanistic approach to personality is most similar to which of the following?
a. radical behaviorism
b. cognitive social learning theories
c. psychoanalytic approaches
d. ancillary analysis approaches
e. none of the above

ANSWER: C
DIFFICULTY LEVEL: M

9.26. An influential existentialist work on the nature of love is:
a. Will May Roll or Love?
b. Roll in Love by Will May
c. Rollo Loves by May Will
d. Love in May by Rollo Will
e. Love and Will by Rollo May

ANSWER: E
DIFFICULTY LEVEL: M

9.27. If you were to enter a school organized by Rousseau, you would likely see
a. boys and girls in gender-segregated classrooms, being reinforced
b. well-behaved children who act "properly" in school
c. children doing all sorts of activities, each learning in his/her own way
d. many toys but no books, as Rousseau believed children should not read
e. children meditating as their teachers read to them from the Bible

ANSWER: C
DIFFICULTY LEVEL: C

9.28. Philosopher Martin Buber called the dialogue in which each human confirms the other person as being of unique value:
a. I'm OK you're OK;
b. action-reaction formation
c. We=we
d. I-Thou
e. You're It.

ANSWER: D
DIFFICULTY LEVEL: M

9.29. According Erich Fromm, love is:
a. an art that enables us to overcome our isolation from others but still maintain our individual integrity
b. an epiphenomenon derived from the sublime pleasure of orgasm
c. the natural outcome of a truly free and uninhibited society
d. a prerequisite for mutual orgasm
e. a pseudo-state invented by Hippies.

ANSWER: A
DIFFICULTY LEVEL: M

9.30. Abraham Maslow called humanistic psychology the:
a. first force
b. second force
c. third force
d. force that is with you
e. "force without force"

ANSWER: C
DIFFICULTY LEVEL: M

9.31. Existentialists sometimes focus on:
a. being-in-the-world
b. positivism
c. the need for basic survival
d. feeling-in-the-world
e. the Annie Hall syndrome

ANSWER: A
DIFFICULTY LEVEL: M

9.32. The idea that people's perceptions or subjective realities are considered to be valid data for investigation is termed:
a. teleology
b. onanism
c. positivism
d. reactionism
e. phenomenology

ANSWER: E
DIFFICULTY LEVEL: C

9.33. Which approach is non-deterministic?
a. psychoanalytic
b. behaviorist
c. ~~existential~~ humanistic
d. biological
e. neo-analytic

ANSWER: C
DIFFICULTY LEVEL: C

9.34. When we are immature and alienated, the world is seen as one big breast, and we are the sucklers. This is the view of:
a. Sigmund Freud
b. Karen Horney
c. B.F. Skinner
d. Erich Fromm
e. David Funder

ANSWER: D
DIFFICULTY LEVEL: M

9.35. In a society that lost cultural traditions to standardized Big Mac hamburgers, and replaced religious concerns about helping others with self-indulgent trips to visit Mickey Mouse, existential/humanists predict that people:
a. will lose the ability for multiple orgasms
b. will feel unified and so less prejudiced
c. should return to orthodox religion
d. would be susceptible to the appeals of totalitarian government
e. need to set up a self-reinforcing environment

ANSWER: D
DIFFICULTY LEVEL: C

9.36. Carl Rogers:
a. grew up on a farm in a religious family environment
b. fled Nazi Europe and converted to Catholicism
c. fled Nazi Europe and renounced all religion as oppressive
d. grew up in the Bronx and got his ideas from the little old ladies who used to gossip on the park benches
e. was deeply inspired as a teen by the Beatles "All you need is love."

ANSWER: A
DIFFICULTY LEVEL: M

9.37. According to Carl Rogers, a psychologically healthy person is one who
a. can totally accept God as the ruler of all things
b. has a broad self-concept that can understand and accept many feelings and experiences
c. is controlled by his environment but doesn't worry about that
d. can overcome penis envy by giving non-sexual gifts to others
e. can function well outside the Bronx, but enjoys home best

ANSWER: B
DIFFICULTY LEVEL: M

9.38. According to an existentialist like Viktor Frankl, an existential struggle can lead to:
a. a triumph of the human spirit
b. a peak orgasm
c. drive reduction
d. a peak construal
e. a taking down of genes

ANSWER: A
DIFFICULTY LEVEL: M

9.39. The process by which one tends to grow spiritually and realize one's potential is called:
a. self-indulgence
b. selflessness
c. self-stimulation
d. liberating the inner homunculus
e. self-actualization

ANSWER: E
DIFFICULTY LEVEL: M

9.40. Maslow called basic biological necessities such as food, water, sex, and shelter, and the need for safety:
a. A-needs
b. B-needs
c. C-needs
d. D-needs
e. E-needs

ANSWER: D
DIFFICULTY LEVEL: C

9.41. In the 1960's and 1970, which approach to personality often meant hippie communes in the woods, with encounter groups, body massage, meditation, organic health foods, and communing with nature?
a. psychoanalytic
b. behaviorist
c. existential/humanistic
d. biological
e. neo-analytic

ANSWER: C
DIFFICULTY LEVEL: E

9.42. In the 1990's, which approach to personality is associated with protecting humans' relations with an unsullied, unpolluted natural eco-sphere, concern with the individual worker's self-development, and concern with the feelings and ideas of small groups of workers?

a. psychoanalytic
b. behaviorist
c. existential/humanistic
d. biological
e. neo-analytic

ANSWER: C
DIFFICULTY LEVEL: M

9.43. Maslow views "higher needs" as:

a. Arising from within the individual
b. Unnecessary in maintaining mental health
c. Unrelated to human value systems except drugs
d. Imposed by the culture of a society
e. Similar to Murray's "Need for Power"

ANSWER: A
DIFFICULTY LEVEL: M

9.44. Which of the below characterize an existentialist's view of human perception?

a. It's more important to understand how a person experiences his/her phenomenology than specific neural mechanisms involved in perception
b. Perception is to some degree dependent on one's needs
c. Perception is to some degree dependent on the meaning an individual attaches to stimuli
d. An individual never really knows what objectively exists
e. All of the above

ANSWER: A
DIFFICULTY LEVEL: M

9.45. Fromm's view of love and society is that...

a. Love is purely a function of the individual's inner experiencing and capacity to self-generalize
b. An individual's ability to love depends on the influence that the culture has on the character of the average person
c. Dopamine re-uptake inhibitors are responsible for increased feelings of love and sexual arousal
d. Freud was essentially correct - love is mostly an irrational phenomenon related to defense mechanisms
e. None of the above

ANSWER: E
DIFFICULTY LEVEL: C

Essay Questions

9.1. Briefly describe Erich Fromm's beliefs about the relationship between inner alienation and having fun. How is it that love can address the problems of human existence?

9.2. Pretend that you are a Rogerian therapist and you are treating a client who has severe test-anxiety and very low self-esteem. Write a short dialogue illustrating what the client might say to you and how you would respond.

9.3. List and briefly describe (in hierarchical order) Maslow's needs.

9.4. What do existentialists mean by the phrase "being-in-the-world"?

9.5. What does the humanistic/existential approach say about free will? How does this conflict with what a behaviorist might say? A Freudian? Which argument do you find to be most compelling?

9.6. How do existentialists reconcile their beliefs about the fundamental human propensity toward growth and fulfillment with ideas of anxiety, dread, and despair?

CHAPTER 10: PERSON-SITUATION INTERACTIONIST ASPECTS

Multiple Choice Questions

10.1. In Hartshorne & May's studies of honesty, it was found that
  a. all of the children stole and cheated when given the opportunity
  b. none of the children stole or cheated when given the opportunity
  c. some children had a "cheating personality"
  d. children who were honest at times were dishonest at other times
  e. none of the above

ANSWER: D
DIFFICULTY LEVEL: M

10.2. The equation B = f(P,E) means
  a. the person and the environment both contribute to behavior
  b. physical education has important implications for mental health
  c. behavior is a function of four factors, only two of which have been proven
  d. an individual will act fundamentally different toward a same-sex individual than toward an opposite-sex individual
  e. none of the above

ANSWER: A
DIFFICULTY LEVEL: C

10.3. For Sullivan, it is most important to examine
  a. what people do when they are alone and unobserved
  b. what people do when they are alone but know they are being observed
  c. how people feel when they have been rejected by others
  d. how extroverts differ physiologically from introverts
  e. how people differ physiologically when they are alone vs. with others

ANSWER: C
DIFFICULTY LEVEL: C

10.4. Mead's idea of the "social self" describes the idea that
  a. the way we see ourselves is determined from our interactions with others
  b. people who are more sociable are more successful in life
  c. people who do not have a "best chum" usually end up with brain damage
  d. people who do not have a "best chum" usually end up with emotional problems
  e. none of the above

ANSWER: A
DIFFICULTY LEVEL: C

10.5. Sullivan integrated many ideas from which two individuals?
  a. Sapir and Freud
  b. Freud and Thorndike
  c. Thorndike and Mead
  d. Thorndike and Sapir
  e. Mead and Sapir

ANSWER: E
DIFFICULTY LEVEL: C

10.6. Julian was always something of a "screw-up" in school. His grades were poor and he was suspended several times during high school for pulling pranks that his teachers didn't find funny. His parents were pleasantly surprised, however, when he went off to college. He enjoyed his biology classes so much that he decided to become a doctor —and he began getting As in all of his classes! His friends in college were the "intellectuals" and he spent many late nights at a local coffee house discussing politics and ethical issues related to the practice of medicine. After a successful first year, his parents were amazed to see him slip back into his slovenly habits and jokester ways when he returned home for the summer. Julian's behavior best illustrates the ideas of which personality theorist?
  a. Horney
  b. Skinner
  c. Piaget
  d. Sullivan
  e. Rotter

ANSWER: D
DIFFICULTY LEVEL: M

10.7. Who coined the term "personology"?
a. Sullivan
b. Murray
c. Lewin
d. Jung
e. Mischel

ANSWER: B
DIFFICULTY LEVEL: M

10.8. According to Murray, _______ are internal motivations and the power of the situation is called ________.
a. desires; behaviors
b. needs; behaviors
c. desires; needs
d. needs; press
e. intuitions; needs

ANSWER: D
DIFFICULTY LEVEL: M

10.9. Murray's measurement tool, designed to assess "thema" is called the
a. the M. A. California Psychological Inventory
b. Life Orientation Theme Test
c. Social Readjustment Rating Scale
d. Rorschach Inkblot Test
e. Thematic Apperception Test

ANSWER: E
DIFFICULTY LEVEL: E

10.10. You arrive at a new therapist's office and are told that you will be given several assessments in order to help the therapist understand you better. The first thing the therapist does is show you a series of pictures and asks you to tell the "story" of what is taking place in the picture. The therapist is probably administering the
a. Q-sort
b. CPI
c. TAT
d. MMPI
e. MPQ

ANSWER: C
DIFFICULTY LEVEL: E

10.11. Mischel's basic argument (that began a great controversy) was that
a. there is no such thing as "personality"
b. knowing someone's personality traits does not allow one to predict that person's behavior in a particular situation
c. it is futile to look at the situation because behavior is almost completely determined by a person's traits
d. the correlations between personality traits and behaviors are so high that it is redundant to study them both
e. none of the above

ANSWER: B
DIFFICULTY LEVEL: C

10.12. Mischel stated that correlations between personality traits and behavior were
a. almost always below .30
b. usually ranged from .50 to .70
c. usually ranged from .70 to .80
d. routinely scattered everywhere from .20 to .90
e. always in the .30 to .60 range

ANSWER: A
DIFFICULTY LEVEL: C

10.13. What does it mean when two behaviors are functionally equivalent?
a. they are the exact same behavior occurring in different geographic locations
b. they both take the same amount of energy
c. they are different behaviors, but derive from the same underlying motivation
d. they both involve interactions with the same group of people
e. none of the above

ANSWER: C
DIFFICULTY LEVEL: M

10.14. When comparing the correlation between personality and behavior with the correlation between situation and behavior, we find that
a. the situation is a better predictor of behavior
b. the personality is a better predictor of behavior
c. neither the situation nor the personality contribute to the prediction of behavior
d. both the situation and the personality contribute about equally to the prediction of behavior
e. none of the above

ANSWER: D
DIFFICULTY LEVEL: C

10.15. Which of the following does NOT influence an individual's ability to delay gratification?
a. visibility of the desired object
b. modeling
c. distraction
d. generation
e. none of the above—all influence delay of gratification

ANSWER: D
DIFFICULTY LEVEL: E

10.16. According to Mischel, encoding strategies are
a. our abilities and knowledge
b. the mechanisms we use to process information
c. our expectations of personality ability
d. our expectations about the consequences of our behaviors
e. the plans we make

ANSWER: B
DIFFICULTY LEVEL: C

10.17. It is often easy to believe stereotypes because
a. we don't see people in a wide variety of situations, so we assume they ARE the way we usually see them
b. they are usually completely true
c. people try to present themselves in stereotypical ways
d. all of the above
e. none of the above

ANSWER: A
DIFFICULTY LEVEL: M

10.18. In general, people tend to __________ the consistency of their own behaviors.
a. be accurate about
b. overestimate
c. underestimate
d. purposely lie about
e. none of the above

ANSWER: B
DIFFICULTY LEVEL: E

10.19. People are better at judging the personalities of others
a. when they know them well
b. when they have seen them in only a few situations
c. when they don't know them at all
d. when they like them
e. when they dislike them

ANSWER: A
DIFFICULTY LEVEL: M

10.20. Which of the following are examples of the power of situational factors in determining behavior?
a. panic arising when a movie theater catches fire
b. "good" people engaging in illegal activities during the 1960s
c. decent Germans cooperating with the diabolical plans of the Nazis
d. all of the above
e. none of the above

ANSWER: D
DIFFICULTY LEVEL: E

10.21. The correlation between personality and behavior is higher when
a. behavior is averaged across situations
b. only a single instance of behavior is measured
c. physiological tools are used to measure behavior
d. the personality trait is not relevant to the behavior
e. none of the above

ANSWER: A
DIFFICULTY LEVEL: C

10.22. People who are more field independent are likely to be ____________ in their behaviors across situations, as compared with those that are field dependent.
a. more consistent
b. less consistent
c. less happy
d. less depressed
e. more insincere

ANSWER: A
DIFFICULTY LEVEL: C

10.23. What is a longitudinal study?
- a. a study in which people are given lengthy forms to fill out for assessment purposes
- b. a study in which people are moved from place to place by researchers so that they can be observed in a variety of situations
- c. a study in which people are observed and studied over significant portions of their life spans
- d. a study in which people are constantly presented with questions that have counter-intuitive answers
- e. a study in which people do not know they are being studied

ANSWER: C
DIFFICULTY LEVEL: E

10.24. Which of the following is not one of the types of data collected by the Blocks in their longitudinal study?
- a. life data
- b. test data
- c. observational data
- d. self-report data
- e. contradictory data

ANSWER: E
DIFFICULTY LEVEL: M

10.25. The study of personality across the "life course" or "life path" takes into account which of the following influences of behavior?
- a. traits and motives
- b. age and life events
- c. culture and social groups
- d. abilities and drives
- e. all of the above

ANSWER: E
DIFFICULTY LEVEL: C

10.26. The adage "You can't teach an old dog new tricks" can be applied to a person-by-situation interaction perspective to reflect which of the concepts below?
a. experience has its effect in the context of previous experiences
b. we are more affected by certain environments at certain times in our lives
c. once we reach a certain age we cannot learn anything new
d. experience has its effect in the context of previous experiences and we are also more affected by certain environments at certain times in our lives
e. experience has its effect in the context of previous experiences, but if we have not had a learning experience in the past year, we will be unable to learn new tricks

ANSWER: D
DIFFICULTY LEVEL: C

10.27. Lorenz found that during a critical period, ducklings will ________ on their mother (or whoever is available).
a. imprint
b. reprint
c. implant
d. impose
e. none of the above

ANSWER: A
DIFFICULTY LEVEL: E

10.28. Which of the following may affect our susceptibility to environmental influences?
a. our past experiences
b. our personality traits
c. circadian rhythms
d. all of the above
e. none of the above

ANSWER: D
DIFFICULTY LEVEL: M

10.29. It seems that small-group interactions can be categorized into which two broad dimensions?
a. affiliation and loneliness
b. affiliation and assertiveness
c. assertiveness and loneliness
d. loneliness and generosity
e. generosity and affiliation

ANSWER: B
DIFFICULTY LEVEL: M

10.30. According to Loevinger, undeveloped egos are often
a. impulsive, self-protective, or conformist
b. generous, unselfish, or gregarious
c. individualistic, autonomous, or integrated
d. all of the above
e. none of the above

ANSWER: A
DIFFICULTY LEVEL: C

10.31. Imagine a boy, whose needs for love and tenderness are not being met by his mother, and who is a Catholic growing up in a prejudiced Protestant farming community, and who has the pressures of a boy with homosexual feelings growing up in an aggressively heterosexual world. This describes:
a. Walter Mischel
b. Abraham Maslow
c. Harry Sullivan
d. Erik Erikson
e. Albert Bandura

ANSWER: C
DIFFICULTY LEVEL: C

10.32. Murray's Needs include which one of the following:
a. Need for Transcendence
b. Need for Exhibition
c. Need for Multiple Orgasm
d. Need for Death (thanatos)
e. Need for Inner Pain (IP)

ANSWER: B
DIFFICULTY LEVEL: C

10.33. A "cheating personality" cannot generally be found. This is because:

a. It is a cross between Conscientiousness and Openness
b. Human nature generally strives to be honest
c. Honesty depends so much on the Superego
d. Honesty depends so much on the situation
e. Honesty depends so much on natural selection processes

ANSWER: D
DIFFICULTY LEVEL: M

10.34. Personality is the relatively enduring pattern of recurrent interpersonal situations that characterize a person's life. This is the view of:

a. Henry Murray
b. Harry Sullivan
c. B. F. Skinner
d. Carl Rogers
e. Roger Will

ANSWER: B
DIFFICULTY LEVEL: M

10.35. John recently brought his TA a box of cookies. To determine the traits relevant to this act and the meaning of this act, Funder would suggest that you would want to know

a. What the TA thinks of John and what John thinks of the TA
b. The immediate situation and John's past behavior with TA's
c. John's grade point average
d. John's level of Need for Achievement
e. How incongruent John is from his "real self" and his level of self-actualization

ANSWER: B
DIFFICULTY LEVEL: C

10.36. The ethological idea of "readiness," as applied to understanding the interaction of the person and the situation, implies that:

a. when the male is ready to mate, other considerations become secondary
b. that we are not ready to act until we can interact
c. that the dance of the stickleback and the pheromones of insects have their counterparts in any disco or singles bar
d. that women signal their readiness with blushed lips when the time is right
e. that we are more affected by certain environments at certain times in our lives

ANSWER: E
DIFFICULTY LEVEL: E

10.37. The primary idea behind an interactionist perspective is that

a. an extrovert will always behave in an identifiably extroverted manner
b. certain situations lead to identical behavior in introverts and extroverts
c. personality can only be appropriately judged in the context of interpersonal interaction
d. people's relationships with one another are a consequence of childhood behavior patterns
e. observed behavior results from a mix of situational and dispositional causes

ANSWER: E
DIFFICULTY LEVEL: E

Essay Questions

10.1. Why does it make sense to study personality, even though correlations between measured personality and behavior in specific situations are often quite low?

10.2. Assume that Judy is introverted and shy. You watch Judy arrive at a party and park her car in the driveway. Briefly describe two things that she might do next which, although behaviorally different, would be functionally equivalent.

10.3. If you are really craving a bag of potato chips but you know you need to stick to your diet, you will try to delay gratification— that is, you will try NOT to eat the potato chips (which would no doubt taste wonderful and be quite rewarding) so that you will feel attractive in your bathing suit next weekend (which is even more wonderful and rewarding). Describe two tactics you might use to make your delay of gratification easier.

10.4 It is unfortunately common for student riots to occur on or near college campuses, especially in April and May. Describe how the concept of "the power of the situation" can explain such behavior by intelligent and well educated people.

CHAPTER 11: MALE-FEMALE DIFFERENCES

Multiple Choice Questions

11.1. Biological characteristics determine ________; ________ is socially constructed.

a. sex; gender
b. masculinity; femininity
c. gender; sex;
d. femininity; masculinity
e. sexuality; sex

ANSWER: A
DIFFICULTY LEVEL: M

11.2. Which of the following is NOT a traditionally masculine characteristic?

a. assertiveness
b. boldness
c. instrumentality
d. nurturance
e. action

ANSWER: D
DIFFICULTY LEVEL: E

11.3. Which of the following is NOT a traditionally feminine characteristic?

a. emotionality
b. cooperativeness
c. sensitivity
d. caring
e. dominance

ANSWER: E
DIFFICULTY LEVEL: M

11.4. In Broverman's 1972 study of perceptions of men and women, it was found that
  a. men and women were perceived to differ on only five personality characteristics
  b. men and women were not perceived to differ in terms of personality characteristics
  c. both men and women perceived masculine characteristics to be more desirable than feminine characteristics
  c. men and women were perceived to differ on over 400 personality characteristics
  d. none of the above

  ANSWER: C
  DIFFICULTY LEVEL: E

11.5. The statement "there is substantial overlap between the distributions of male and female traits and behaviors" means that
  a. men and women share a few traits
  b. men and women share a few behaviors
  c. although there may be group differences between males and females in traits and behaviors, there are lots of men that score higher than lots of women on "feminine" traits and behaviors, and vice versa
  d. all of the above
  e. none of the above

  ANSWER: C
  DIFFICULTY LEVEL: M

11.6. Which of the following male-female "differences" does **not** exist?
  a. males commit more violent crimes than females
  b. girls, on average, learn to talk earlier than boys do
  c. boys, on average, do better on tasks requiring spatial abilities than girls do
  d. females tend to be more sensitive to nonverbal cues than are males
  e. females are more psychologically sensitive than are males

  ANSWER: E
  DIFFICULTY LEVEL: M

11.7. Which of the following individuals believed women to be inferior to men?
  a. Plato
  b. Aristotle
  c. Thomas Aquinas
  d. all of the above
  e. none of the above

  ANSWER: D
  DIFFICULTY LEVEL: E

11.8. In ancient petroglyphs and hieroglyphs, men were usually portrayed as
- a. fathers or husbands
- b. warriors or hunters
- c. builders
- d. animals
- e. monks

ANSWER: B
DIFFICULTY LEVEL: E

11.9. What evidence supports the idea that prenatal exposure to androgen might affect personality as well as physical development?
- a. studies of animals whose exposure to prenatal androgen has been experimentally altered
- b. studies of humans whose exposure to prenatal androgen has been experimentally altered
- c. studies of humans who have experienced prenatal genetic or hormonal anomalies
- d. a and c
- e. none of the above

ANSWER: D
DIFFICULTY LEVEL: M

11.10. If you are presented with two cages of rats (each cage contains both males and females), and the rats in one cage seem much more aggressive and active, you might hypothesize that
- a. the rats in this cage were prenatally exposed to extra estrogen
- b. the rats in this cage were prenatally exposed to extra androgen
- c. the rats in this cage were fed a high-fat diet
- d. the rats in this cage were deprived of sleep
- e. the rats in this cage were postnatally exposed to serotonin

ANSWER: B
DIFFICULTY LEVEL: M

11.11. There is some evidence that individuals with Turner's syndrome are
- a. more timid than other women
- b. more aggressive than other women
- c. more mathematically- and spatially-adept than other women
- d. more generous than other women
- e. more verbal than other women

ANSWER: A
DIFFICULTY LEVEL: C

11.12. Women's hormonal cycles have been said to be associated with
a. mood swings
b. indecisiveness
c. violence
d. all of the above
e. none of the above

ANSWER: D
DIFFICULTY LEVEL: M

11.13. The influence of hormonal cycles on personality in women is
a. large
b. moderate
c. small
d. unknown, it has not yet been studied
e. although this has been studied, no information has been reported

ANSWER: C
DIFFICULTY LEVEL: M

11.14. If you were dissecting two human brains, one male and one female, you might expect to find
a. that the female brain's left hemisphere was larger
b. that the female brain's right hemisphere was larger
c. that the female brain's corpus callosum was larger
d. that the female brain was larger
e. none of the above

ANSWER: C
DIFFICULTY LEVEL: M

11.15. Why did Freud assert that "anatomy is destiny"?
a. because we cannot change our sex
b. because ultimately we identify with our same-sex parent
c. because he believed that different races should not intermarry
d. all of the above
e. none of the above

ANSWER: B
DIFFICULTY LEVEL: M

11.16. Which theorist placed an emphasis on recognizing and incorporating both "maleness" and "femaleness" into healthy human development (that is, the concept of androgyny)?
a. Freud
b. Horney
c. Jung
d. Erikson
e. Skinner

ANSWER: C
DIFFICULTY LEVEL: M

11.17. The statement "men can't be faithful to just one woman-- it's not in their nature" implies
a. an evolutionary approach
b. a psychoanalytic approach
c. a neoanalytic approach
d. a behaviorist approach
e. a cognitive approach

ANSWER: A
DIFFICULTY LEVEL: M

11.18. A non-parental rat received an injection and then began to exhibit maternal behavior. The injection could have been
a. a saline solution
b. testosterone
c. blood from a female rat that recently gave birth
d. either testosterone or blood from a female rat that recently gave birth
e. norepinephrine

ANSWER: D
DIFFICULTY LEVEL: C

11.19. Maslow posited that a self-actualized person would have
a. only traditionally-feminine characteristics
b. only traditionally-masculine characteristics
c. both traditionally-feminine and traditionally-masculine characteristics
d. all of the above
e. none of the above

ANSWER: C
DIFFICULTY LEVEL: M

11.20. According to the humanistic perspective, gender differences in personality will _________ as societies equalize opportunities for men and women.
a. become larger
b. become smaller
c. remain the same
d. fluctuate widely
e. none of the above

ANSWER: B
DIFFICULTY LEVEL: C

11.21. Which of the following is an example of the social learning of gender-related norms?
a. Tom's father teaches him to work on the car
b. Brian's mom scolds him for being a sissy when he is picked on by others and doesn't retaliate
c. Gene's older brothers encourage him to join in their tackle-football games but tell their younger sister Julie that she can't play
d. all of the above
e. none of the above

ANSWER: D
DIFFICULTY LEVEL: E

11.22. Which of the following is NOT an example of a gender schema?
a. a kind person would never hurt an animal
b. it's not appropriate for girls to call boys on the phone
c. when going to the prom, boys should wear tuxedos and girls should wear gowns
d. loud and sassy women are not attractive to men
e. only a weak man cries

ANSWER: A
DIFFICULTY LEVEL: M

11.23. In current theorizing, masculinity and femininity are conceptualized as
a. opposite poles of one dimension
b. separate dimensions
c. the same as "male" and "female"
d. all of the above
e. none of the above

ANSWER: B
DIFFICULTY LEVEL: M

11.24. Erik is an excellent student, excels in math, and enjoys spelling. He is gregarious and has lots of friends. Often, he is a group leader, directing other children and coordinating their games. He is also sensitive, and is often sought out for advice or just a "listening ear." Based on this brief description, Erik would probably score as _________ on the Bem Sex Role Inventory.

a. masculine
b. feminine
c. undifferentiated
d. androgynous
e. none of the above

ANSWER: D
DIFFICULTY LEVEL: M

11.25. Marcia loves sports and is fiercely competitive. She's played soccer since she was seven, and since starting high school has become a track and field star. Some of Marcia's friends describe her as "tough" although they are quick to add that she always has fun. Although her friendships are not deep, Marcia is extremely popular and almost everyone in school knows her name. Marcia hopes to be an engineer one day. Based on this brief description, Marcia would probably score as ___________ on the Bem Sex Role Inventory.

a. masculine
b. feminine
c. androgynous
d. undifferentiated
e. none of the above

ANSWER: A
DIFFICULTY LEVEL: E

11.26. Men generally are found to have more "dominant" personalities when dominance is defined as

a. aggression
b. affiliation
c. leadership
d. all of the above
e. none of the above

ANSWER: A
DIFFICULTY LEVEL: M

11.27. When it is found that men are less emotional than women, one possible explanation might be

a. that men are genetically programmed to be less emotional
b. that society teaches men to hide their emotions
c. that differences in emotionality are cultural myths that influence our perceptions of emotionality
d. all of the above
e. none of the above

ANSWER: D
DIFFICULTY LEVEL: M

11.28. When babies and preschoolers are observed, ________ cry most; when older children and adults are observed, ________ cry most.

a. boys; girls
b. girls; boys
c. girls; girls
d. boys; boys
e. neither boys nor girls; girls

ANSWER: A
DIFFICULTY LEVEL: M

11.29. Andrea wants to be famous-- she works hard in her classes and gets straight As; she attends workshops and conferences in her field and makes an effort to meet all the right people; during the summer she volunteers many hours at a research lab. She is sure that nothing will stand in her way. McClelland would say that Andrea is

a. low on social status
b. high on achievement motivation
c. high on sensation-seeking
d. low on conscientiousness
e. high on need for affiliation

ANSWER: B
DIFFICULTY LEVEL: M

11.30. A study that examines helping-behavior by placing people in an experimental situation where they must decide whether to take a risk and help a stranger in need will probably show that
a. men help more often than women do
b. women help more often than men do
c. men and women are equal in their helping behavior
d. neither men nor women will help
e. impossible to predict

ANSWER: A
DIFFICULTY LEVEL: C

11.31. Empirically, girls and women have been shown to be more likely than boys
a. to seek social contact with others
b. to be sensitive to social situations
c. to be verbally aggressive
d. all of the above
e. none of the above

ANSWER: E
DIFFICULTY LEVEL: C

11.32. As a group, women have been found to be better than men at
a. decoding facial and body cues
b. recognizing faces
c. expressing themselves nonverbally
d. all of the above
e. none of the above

ANSWER: D
DIFFICULTY LEVEL: M

11.33. A study of courtship among Boston college students found that
a. men were more devastated when relationships ended
b. men were more likely to be "broken up with" than to "break up with" their partners
c. men had more romantic ideas than women and seemed to "love" more in the relationship
d. all of the above
e. none of the above

ANSWER: D
DIFFICULTY LEVEL: C

11.34. In some times in some societies, girls were (and sometimes still are) given clitoridectomies (genital mutilations) in order to prevent their "insatiable and shameful" sexual drives. This suggests that current American views (and studies) showing men with greater sex drives are likely the result of:

a. culture-specific gender stereotypes
d. Madonna repression syndrome
c. repressed penis envy
d. the influence of Dr. Ruth
e. androgyny

ANSWER: A
DIFFICULTY LEVEL: M

Essay Questions

11.1. What is the difference between "sex" and "gender"? What do the terms "masculinity" and "femininity" mean? How do these terms fit in with "sex" and "gender"?

11.2. What are two broad areas of research that lead us to believe that some behavioral/personality characteristics may be biologically (genetically/hormonally) determined? Give one specific example of research that points to this conclusion.

11.3. In cases where one's genetic sex (XX vs. XY) does not match one's external genitalia, one might be raised in accordance with one's outward appearance. How does the fact that this is often quite successful speak to the power of socialization and expectations in gender formation?

11.4. How might the psychoanalytic approach to personality be viewed as biologically-based?

11.5. Give one example of how a gender difference in sexual behavior might be classically conditioned.

11.6. Briefly describe how the profile of a female leader might be different from that of a male leader.

CHAPTER 12: STRESS, ADJUSTMENT, AND HEALTH DIFFERENCES

Multiple Choice Questions

12.1. Underlying psychosomatic medicine is the idea that
   a. medications can be used to treat psychiatric disorders
   b. the mind is capable of affecting the body
   c. medicine should be used to treat illnesses that are "all in one's head"
   d. medications are relatively useless because illness is a mental state
   e. none of the above

   ANSWER: B
   DIFFICULTY LEVEL: M

12.2. Which of the following sets up the scenario for a link between personality and health via health behaviors?
   a. Jeannette is often depressed and lethargic
   b. Jeannette is an anxious person and often calms herself by smoking
   c. Jeannette is a very religious person
   d. Jeannette is extremely extroverted and often attends parties
   e. Jeannette enjoys spending time with her children and has a good sense of humor

   ANSWER: B
   DIFFICULTY LEVEL: M

12.3. Smoking and drinking have been linked to which of the following personality characteristics?
   a. rebelliousness
   b. aggressiveness
   c. impulsivity
   d. alienation
   e. all of the above

   ANSWER: E
   DIFFICULTY LEVEL: C

12.4. Which of the following is NOT a subscale of Zuckerman's "sensation seeking"?
a. thrill and adventure seeking
b. experience seeking
c. social-support seeking
d. disinhibition
e. boredom susceptibility

ANSWER: C
DIFFICULTY LEVEL: C

12.5. In a study by Furnham & Saipe, it was found that fast, reckless drivers scored higher than "good drivers" on ____________.
a. Zuckerman's sensation-seeking and Eysenck's psychoticism
b. Zuckerman's sensation-seeking and Scheier & Carver's optimism
c. Scheier & Carver's optimism and Costa & McCrae's neuroticism
d. Beck's depression and Costa & McCrae's neuroticism
e. Eysenck's psychoticism and Costa & McCrae's neuroticism

ANSWER: A
DIFFICULTY LEVEL: C

12.6. Farley's "Type T" is most similar to which of the following?
a. Type A
b. Type B
c. Type C
d. sensation-seeking
e. shyness

ANSWER: D
DIFFICULTY LEVEL: M

12.7. Of the following, who has entered the "sick role"?
a. Andrew has HIV but doesn't know it; he lives his life as usual
b. Nancy was recently diagnosed with cancer but she refuses to accept it; she works full-time, goes out with friends, and hasn't told anybody
c. Matt mopes around the house and sleeps a lot-- he is convinced that he has Epstein-Barr Virus or perhaps Chronic Fatigue Syndrome; the doctors haven't been able to make a diagnosis
d. all of the above have entered the sick role
e. none of the above have entered the sick role

ANSWER: C
DIFFICULTY LEVEL: M

12.8. According to Skinnerian theory, some of the reinforcers which encourage adoption of the sick role might be
a. attention
b. sympathy
c. days off from work
d. all of the above
e. none of the above

ANSWER: D
DIFFICULTY LEVEL: E

12.9. Which of the following can affect symptom reporting?
a. depression
b. anxiety
c. neuroticism
d. all of the above
e. none of the above

ANSWER: D
DIFFICULTY LEVEL: M

12.10. In the 1940s study of Johns Hopkins medical students, which temperament was found to be the biggest risk factor for serious health problems and even death?
a. slow and solid
b. rapid and facile
c. irregular and uneven
d. all of the above
e. none of the above

ANSWER: C
DIFFICULTY LEVEL: C

12.11. June has a history of skin problems, and as a teenager she had severe acne. Her breakouts are now controlled, but when she gets stressed out her acne flares up. This is an example of
a. the reactance model
b. the diathesis-stress model
c. the reciprocity model
d. the operational-diagnosis model
e. the vulnerability-diametric model

ANSWER: B
DIFFICULTY LEVEL: C

12.12. Lown believes that sudden cardiac death is preceded by all but which of the following?
a. electrical instability
b. pervasive negative emotions (depression)
c. a previous heart attack
d. a triggering event
e. none of the above

ANSWER: C
DIFFICULTY LEVEL: C

12.13. In the 1950s study of Western Electrical Company employees, which of the following was found to be a risk factor for cancer deaths?
a. excessive optimism
b. depression
c. hostility
d. conscientiousness
e. being a workaholic

ANSWER: B
DIFFICULTY LEVEL: C

12.14. Associations between personality and cancer have been found to be
a. extremely robust
b. moderate
c. quite weak
d. all of the above
e. none of the above

ANSWER: C
DIFFICULTY LEVEL: M

12.15. Who coined the term "Type A Behavior Pattern"?
a. Menninger & Menninger
b. Rosenman & Friedman
c. Alexander & Zuckerman
d. Farley & Dunbar
e. Glass & Seligman

ANSWER: B
DIFFICULTY LEVEL: C

12.16. Someone who has "learned helplessness" will
a. wait patiently in a bad situation until the right moment comes to escape
b. attack aggressively at the first sign that someone is trying to force him or her to become helpless
c. remain in a bad situation even when there is a way to escape it
d. someone with learned helpless would be likely to do any of these
e. someone with learned helplessness would not do any of these

ANSWER: C
DIFFICULTY LEVEL: M

12.17. When retirement means giving up an interesting routine, prestige, and an enjoyable social life, it's likely to be _________; when it means free time to pursue hobbies, a chance to relax, and more quality time with family, it's likely to be ____________.
a. healthy; healthy
b. unhealthy; healthy
c. healthy; unhealthy
d. unhealthy; unhealthy
e. impossible to predict

ANSWER: B
DIFFICULTY LEVEL: E

12.18. In Friedman & Booth-Kewley's meta-analysis on personality and various diseases,
a. there seems to be a generic "disease prone" personality
b. anxiety is related to asthma and ulcers, but not heart disease
c. there is no evidence for a "disease prone" personality
d. depression is related to cancer but not to other illnesses
e. depression is related to arthritis but not to other diseases

ANSWER: A
DIFFICULTY LEVEL: M

12.19. Terman began his longitudinal study of bright children in
b. the 1940s a. the 1920s

c. the 1960s
d. the 1980s
e. the 1990s

ANSWER: A
DIFFICULTY LEVEL: M

12.20. Using the Terman archives, Friedman and his colleagues found that _______ children tended to live longer, while ________ children tended to die earlier.
a. cheerful; sociable
b. cheerful; neurotic
c. conscientious; cheerful
d. sociable; neurotic
e. neurotic; conscientious

ANSWER: C
DIFFICULTY LEVEL: M

12.21. The link between experiencing parental divorce as a child and subsequent mortality risk has been shown to be partially explained by
a. the increased rate of marital breakup in those who have experienced parental divorce
b. the increased level of openness in those who have experienced parental divorce
c. the decreased ability to sleep restfully in those who have experienced parental divorce
d. all of the above
e. none of the above

ANSWER: A
DIFFICULTY LEVEL: C

12.22. What is one reason it's sometimes tempting to "blame the victim" for his/her illness?
a. we don't like victims
b. we crave an unpredictable world
c. we desire a predictable world
d. we don't want to take personal responsibility
e. none of the above

ANSWER: C
DIFFICULTY LEVEL: M

12.23. Which of the following is NOT a characteristic of Kobasa & Maddi's "hardiness"?
a. aggression
b. control
c. commitment
d. challenge
e. none of the above

ANSWER: A
DIFFICULTY LEVEL: M

12.24. Rotter's work on "locus of control" is well-known, but his writings about _______ have been largely ignored by personality psychologists.

a. ingenuity
b. trust
c. intelligence
d. hypnotism
e. acupuncture

ANSWER: B
DIFFICULTY LEVEL: M

12.25. A placebo is

a. an experimental drug
b. a very strong and powerful drug
c. an uncommon and little known drug
d. a drug which simultaneously exerts two opposite effects
e. an inert substance that nonetheless affects physical health

ANSWER: E
DIFFICULTY LEVEL: E

12.26. Which of the following individuals best portrays a self-healing personality?

a. Alicia is constantly on the go—and she always wants to be the best and to efficiently accomplish more in less time
b. Pamela is constantly on the go—and she loves her work and never seems to get tired
c. Brent is quiet and shy—he doesn't seem to "match" with his siblings who are all very outgoing, and in the past this has made him feel badly about himself, so he now tries very hard to be outgoing and gain more friends
d. Ian is kind of boorish but nobody will ever take advantage of him, because he is constantly on the offensive, and has no anxiety
e. Petra worries about everything, but she is able to put it out of her mind and walk around with a smile on her face

ANSWER: B
DIFFICULTY LEVEL: M

Essay Questions

12.1. Some studies have shown that hostility is a risk factor for heart disease and that depression is a risk factor for cancer. Why is it that we cannot say that depression causes cancer or that hostility causes heart disease?

12.2. What does it mean to say that a risk factor is neither a necessary nor a sufficient cause for disease?

12.3. What are the potential ramifications (both positive and negative) of linking physical health to behavioral factors? What about linking physical health to personality traits?

12.4. Briefly describe the two broad types of self-healing personalities. What does it mean to say that the personality-environment match is of paramount importance?

12.5. How do behaviors provide a link between personality and health? What is one other link, as discussed in the textbook?

CHAPTER 13: CULTURAL AND ETHNIC DIFFERENCES

Multiple Choice Questions

13.1. Although cultural and ethnic aspects of personality have often been ignored, ________ was studying the impact of the experiences of Blacks and Jews in the 1950s.
a. Freud
b. Adler
c. Allport
d. Bandura
e. Sullivan

ANSWER: C
DIFFICULTY LEVEL: M

13.2. Measuring everyone against the norms and customs of one's own ethnic group is termed
a. ethnocentrism
b. ethnography
c. transethnicity
d. ethological
e. none of the above

ANSWER: A
DIFFICULTY LEVEL: M

13.3. Mead, in her study of South Pacific Islanders, found that
a. the difficulties of adolescence are the same across cultures
b. the difficulties of adolescence are not the same across cultures
c. in some cultures there is no hormonal puberty
d. in some cultures adolescents are viewed as gods
e. none of the above

ANSWER: B
DIFFICULTY LEVEL: M

13.4. According to research by Whiting & Whiting, children who grow up in a cooperative home environment tend to be more ________ as adults than those raised in a competitive, "me first" atmosphere.
a. antisocial
b. extroverted
c. prosocial
d. introverted
e. neurotic

ANSWER: C
DIFFICULTY LEVEL: M

13.5. Linton, in his book, The Cultural Background of Personality, argues that
a. people in the same culture all share the same personality traits
b. people in the same culture share things like behavior and knowledge, which may mold apparent "personality"
c. personality is set in early childhood by the influence of key figures in the culture
d. all of the above
e. none of the above

ANSWER: B
DIFFICULTY LEVEL: M

13.6. A(n) _______ approach to personality focuses on one culture, whereas a(n) _______ approach is cross-cultural.
a. rational; diverse
b. narrow; emic
c. etic; emic
d. emic; etic
e. etic; rational

ANSWER: D
DIFFICULTY LEVEL: C

13.7. Cross-cultural researchers have found that Western cultures tend to be more _________ whereas Eastern cultures emphasize a(n) ___________ viewpoint.
a. humanitarian; individualistic
b. individualistic; collectivist
c. collectivist; outspoken
d. outspoken; optimistic
e. optimistic; pessimistic

ANSWER: B
DIFFICULTY LEVEL: M

13.8. Groups are often formed based on which of the following?
a. political and religious beliefs
b. customs and behaviors
c. physical characteristics
d. all of the above
e. none of the above

ANSWER: D
DIFFICULTY LEVEL: M

13.9. The "American Dilemma" as discussed by Myrdal, refers to
a. the fact that Americans believe that "all men are created equal" and yet, everyone is not treated equally
b. that individuals have the right to "life, liberty, and the pursuit of happiness" and yet people often die early in life, before having a chance to really "live"
c. that the "American Dream" is to own a house and raise a family and yet it is becoming harder and harder to achieve this goal
d. all of the above
e. none of the above

ANSWER: A
DIFFICULTY LEVEL: M

13.10. Socioeconomic status (SES) is a term that describes a person's relative standing in
a. education and physical characteristics
b. income and physical characteristics
c. ancestry and income
d. ancestry and physical characteristics
e. education and income

ANSWER: E
DIFFICULTY LEVEL: E

13.11. The fact that someone with higher SES is at a lower risk of becoming ill and dying prematurely than someone of lower SES is called
a. the SES bias
b. the SES gradient
c. the SES enigma
d. the SES injustice
e. the SES condition

ANSWER: B
DIFFICULTY LEVEL: M

13.12. According to Marx, psychosocial phenomena such as alienation could be understood by studying
a. the economic structure of capitalist societies
b. personality traits across cultures
c. great leaders of socialist societies
d. the criminal minds of convicted killers
e. none of the above

ANSWER: A
DIFFICULTY LEVEL: E

13.13. Features of language that are common to all languages are called
a. tongues
b. linguistics
c. linguistic universals
d. vocal norms
d. audio-consistencies

ANSWER: C
DIFFICULTY LEVEL: M

13.14. Which of the following aspect of language, according to your textbook, is a facet of personality?
a. vocabulary
b. dialect
c. intellect
d. idiolect
e. none of the above

ANSWER: D
DIFFICULTY LEVEL: C

13.15. Which of the following illustrates how closely people associate their identity with their language?
a. the "English only" movement in the U.S.
b. bilingual education
c. cross-cultural psychology
d. all of the above
e. none of the above

ANSWER: A
DIFFICULTY LEVEL: M

13.16. Language influences all but which of the following?
a. the way we express ourselves
b. the way we think about problems
c. the way we perceive the world
d. the physical characteristics we possess
e. the way we interact with others

ANSWER: D
DIFFICULTY LEVEL: M

13.17. Which of the following illustrates the concept of "linguistic relativity"?
a. Suzy often uses swear words because she hears her older sister swearing
b. Suzy doesn't understand the complexities of weather because, in her culture, words for describing weather are broad and general, rather than specific
c. Suzy speaks differently when she is with close family and relatives than she does when she is around her school friends
d. all of the above
e. none of the above

ANSWER: B
DIFFICULTY LEVEL: C

13.18. Doob has found that people who tend to use active verbs also tend to be
a. field independent
b. field dependent
c. insecure
d. secure
e. open minded

ANSWER: A
DIFFICULTY LEVEL: C

13.19. Social status may be inferred from which of the following
a. age
b. sex
c. wealth
d. occupation
e. all of the above

ANSWER: E
DIFFICULTY LEVEL: E

13.20. Research has shown that a child reading this sentence: "The student was instructed to return his exam to the teacher." is likely to envision __________ if the child is a boy and _________ if the child is a girl.

a. a male student; a female student
b. a female student; a male student
c. a male student; a male student
d. a female student; a female student
e. research on this topic has not been done

ANSWER: C
DIFFICULTY LEVEL: M

13.21. Which of the following assumptions underlies much of psychological testing?

a. "high" scores are better than "low" scores
b. psychological testing never provides any solutions to real-world problems
c. "low" scores are better than "high" scores
d. individuality shines through in psychological testing
e. none of the above

ANSWER: A
DIFFICULTY LEVEL: M

13.22. Scores on psychological tests are known to be affected by

a. previous test-taking experiences
b. cultural experiences
c. qualities of the test administrator
d. motivation
e. all of the above

ANSWER: E
DIFFICULTY LEVEL: E

13.23. Which of the following incorporates culture as part of the assessment itself?

a. System of Multicultural Pluralistic Assessment
b. Raven Progressive Matrices Test
c. Minnesota Multiphasic Personality Inventory
d. all of the above
e. none of the above

ANSWER: A
DIFFICULTY LEVEL: M

13.24. Suppose that you have given a personality test to samples of individuals from two different cultural groups. You find that one group scores significantly higher on neuroticism. How can you determine whether this is a true finding, or whether it reflects a cultural bias in your measurement?

a. have the groups re-take the test and see if the difference still exists
b. have the groups re-take the test after a long period of time and see if the difference still exists
c. look at other sources of information about the groups for confirming or disconfirming evidence
d. ask the individuals if they think the test was biased
e. none of the above would be appropriate

ANSWER: C
DIFFICULTY LEVEL: C

13.25. In Erikson's study of the Sioux in South Dakota, he found that many white teachers believed that the American Indians had fundamental personality flaws (mostly because they didn't cooperate and do well in the classroom). He traced this problem to which of the following?

a. there were independent reservations, but people living on them were dependent on the government for their livelihood
b. lip service was given to "trust" and "cooperation" but promises were often broken
c. American Indian culture was viewed as "different" and yet policies were enacted which forced the norms of the larger American culture onto the American Indians
d. all of the above
e. none of the above

ANSWER: D
DIFFICULTY LEVEL: C

13.26. Brian is a psychologist studying "the psychology of the rave party." He goes to raves in England, Scotland, Canada, and the USA, and records the behavior he observes in each location using one common set of descriptions. Brian is using an _______ approach.

a. enteric
b. emic
c. etic
d. emetic
e. aesthetic

ANSWER: C
DIFFICULTY LEVEL: C

Essay Questions

13.1. Suppose that you have a well-constructed questionnaire that assesses the personality trait "agreeableness." Suppose also that you have demonstrated that your questionnaire does a good job of measuring agreeableness in American college students. Now you want to use your questionnaire to measure agreeableness in a couple of non-English speaking groups (Mexican-American mothers and Vietnamese school children). So, you hire someone to translate your questionnaire into Spanish and Vietnamese. Can you now use this questionnaire? Do you anticipate any problems? If so, what might they be?

13.2. Does it ever make sense to study "race" as it relates to personality? What can we gain from such investigations? What must we be careful to guard against when undertaking these kinds of studies?

13.3. What are some of the mechanisms which might explain the SES gradient? What does the SES gradient have to do with personality?

13.4. People have created language, but how has language served to mold its creators?

13.5. What kinds of tests have been developed that are "culture free?" Are they really free from cultural bias? If not, what kinds of biases still creep in?

CHAPTER 14: LOVE AND HATE

Multiple Choice Questions

14.1. According to the ethological perspective, we are born with the ability to hate because
- a. we all have genetic defects
- b. our ancestors were punished for hating
- c. aggression was selected for through evolution
- d. all of the above
- e. none of the above

ANSWER: C
DIFFICULTY LEVEL: M

14.2. Mass murderers are usually
- a. men in the prime of life
- b. men in their 60s and older
- c. women in the prime of life
- d. women in their 60s and older
- e. none of the above

ANSWER: A
DIFFICULTY LEVEL: E

14.3. What do ethologists believe might cause a buildup of aggression and hatred in individuals?
- a. the lenient atmosphere prevalent in America today
- b. constraints of society and overly strict parents
- c. having a large number of siblings
- d. emphasis on the need for artistic expression in academia
- e. lack of social contact

ANSWER: B
DIFFICULTY LEVEL: M

14.4. The ethologist Lorenz suggests which of the following as a way for people to vent their aggression safely?
a. non-violent arguments
b. spelling competitions
c. counting to ten and taking deep breaths
d. playing sports
e. talking to close friends

ANSWER: D
DIFFICULTY LEVEL: M

14.5. You are at the grocery store and suddenly the person in line behind you goes into a fit of rage: he is yelling, turning red, and his eyes are bugging out (this seems to be an unprovoked rage). If you were told that this person suffers from a brain abnormality the area of the brain that most likely was afftected is
a. the brain stem
b. the temporal lobe
c. the corpus callosum
d. the prefrontal cortex
e. the superior colliculus

ANSWER: B
DIFFICULTY LEVEL: C

14.6. Thanatos is
a. an affiliative drive
b. a self-destructive drive
c. a generative drive
d. a passive drive
e. a parenting drive

ANSWER: B
DIFFICULTY LEVEL: M

14.7. As children, individuals who have anti-social personality disorder often
a. torture animals
b. are cruel to their classmates
c. destroy property
d. all of the above
e. none of the above

ANSWER: D
DIFFICULTY LEVEL: M

14.8. Freudian theory predicts that we might do which of the following with our death instinct?
a. repress it
b. project it
c. displace it
d. all of the above
e. none of the above

ANSWER: D
DIFFICULTY LEVEL: M

14.9. According to Jung, aggression rests in the archetype of
a. the mother
b. the animus
c. the anima
d. the shadow
e. the child-god

ANSWER: D
DIFFICULTY LEVEL: M

14.10. Which Jungian combination would be most likely to characterize an aggressive dictator?
a. thinking-introverted
b. thinking-extroverted
c. feeling-introverted
d. sensing-extroverted
e. intuiting-introverted

ANSWER: B
DIFFICULTY LEVEL: C

14.11. Which child would Adler predict is most likely to become a criminal in adulthood?
a. Joyce was often ill as a child; she had to stay indoors a lot, and although her parents played with her and tried to make her life enjoyable, she didn't have very many friends her own age
b. Shirley was an outgoing child who was always busy; she was an only child, and unplanned since her parents had been told they could never have children; she was the "apple of her parents' eyes" and was quite spoiled throughout childhood
c. Aaron was adopted when he was only two weeks old and considers his adoptive family to be his "true" family; he grew up in a small community where everyone knew everyone else; he grew up feeling that his role in society was important
d. Marie was born into a big family, but since she was the youngest and the only girl her parents favored her; her brothers sometimes picked on her, but she could always run to mom for protection and comfort
e.. Brent was born to a single mother who didn't really want him or have time for him; he never even knew his father, and he grew up feeling rejected by his parents

ANSWER: E
DIFFICULTY LEVEL: M

14.12. Erikson believed that the unsuccessful resolution of childhood conflicts could result in a hostile and hateful adult. Which of the following conflicts did he believe had to be successfully resolved to avoid developing hostility and hate?
a. trust vs. mistrust
b. autonomy vs. shame and doubt
c. initiative vs. guilt
d. all of the above
e. all eight ego crises

ANSWER: D
DIFFICULTY LEVEL: C

14.13. Rogers believed that a lack of ________ was particularly harmful to children.
a. unconditional positive regard
b. conditional positive regard
c. isolation
d. optimizing
e. discipline

ANSWER: A
DIFFICULTY LEVEL: M

14.14. Maslow argued that for optimal development children must
a. feel loved
b. feel safe
c. have rules and structure
d. a and b
e. all of the above

ANSWER: E
DIFFICULTY LEVEL: C

14.15. Which of the following is most likely to be a "cardinal trait" of a serial killer?
a. aggression
b. optimism
c. anxiety
d. helplessness
e. introversion

ANSWER: A
DIFFICULTY LEVEL: M

14.16. Which of the following characteristics help to make up the trait "psychoticism" as described by Eysenck?
a. open-mindedness and optimism
b. generosity and extraversion
c. tough-mindedness and impulsivity
d. all of the above
e. none of the above

ANSWER: C
DIFFICULTY LEVEL: C

14.17. Missy is an ill-behaved little girl. She pulls people's hair, shouts and stomps her feet, and refuses to share her toys. Skinner would argue that in order to understand her aggression we must

a. determine whether her Electra complex has been resolved
b. examine her relationship to her parents (find out if she feels rejected by them)
c. look at her environment to see what elicits aggression and how it is rewarded
d. do blood tests to see if she has some sort of chemical imbalance
e. search for structural abnormalities in her brain

ANSWER: C
DIFFICULTY LEVEL: M

14.18. Freud believed that love was closely linked to

a. friendship
b. sex
c. opportunity
d. all of the above
e. none of the above

ANSWER: B
DIFFICULTY LEVEL: E

14.19. Erikson posits that love becomes a most important issue during the stage of

a. autonomy vs. shame and doubt
b. initiative vs. guilt
c. intimacy vs. isolation
d. generativity vs. stagnation
e. trust vs. mistrust

ANSWER: C
DIFFICULTY LEVEL: C

14.20. Anxious-ambivalent lovers
- a. want relationships but are extremely insecure and desperate
- b. do not want relationships although it sometimes looks like they do
- c. say that they want relationships when in reality they do not
- d. have trouble determining whether they want heterosexual or homosexual partners
- e. are arrogant and overconfident

ANSWER: A
DIFFICULTY LEVEL: M

14.21. According to Maslow, which need must be met first?
- a. need for safety
- b. need for food
- c. need for love
- d. need for self-actualization
- e. none of the above

ANSWER: B
DIFFICULTY LEVEL: M

14.22. Maslow's _________ is the more healthy type.
- a. A-love
- b. B-love
- c. C-love
- d. D-love
- e. E-love

ANSWER: B
DIFFICULTY LEVEL: C

14.23. Which of the following is NOT one of the types of love described by May?
- a. lust
- b. brotherly love
- c. devotion
- d. procreative love
- e. angry love

ANSWER: E
DIFFICULTY LEVEL: M

14.24. According to May, the problem with love in the "hippie" culture was that
a. it was freely given
b. it lacked will
c. it was disciplined
d. it was negative
e. it lacked the element of sexuality

ANSWER: B
DIFFICULTY LEVEL: M

14.25. Lonely people tend to
a. have trouble trusting others
b. have trouble talking about themselves
c. feel uncomfortable in social situations
d. be somewhat low on extraversion
e. all of the above

ANSWER: E
DIFFICULTY LEVEL: M

14.26. Extraverted individuals tend to be __________ sexually than introverts.
a. more adventurous
b. less adventurous
c. more cautious
d. more inhibited
e. less happy

ANSWER: A
DIFFICULTY LEVEL: M

14.27. Who would you predict to be most likely to engage in unsafe sexual practices?
a. someone high on conscientiousness
b. someone high on impulsivity
c. someone high on agreeableness
d. all of the above
e. none of the above

ANSWER: B
DIFFICULTY LEVEL: E

14.28. The Attraction to Sexual Aggression Scale is designed to identify
a. children who have been sexually abused
b. women who use their sexuality to control men
c. men who are likely to engage in sexual violence toward women
d. all of the above
e. none of the above

ANSWER: C
DIFFICULTY LEVEL: E

14.29. According to "The Bell Curve" IQ is highly correlated with
a. income and job success
b. laziness and being on welfare
c. divorce and quality of parenting
d. all of the above
e. none of the above

ANSWER: D
DIFFICULTY LEVEL: C

Essay Questions

14.1. Name and briefly describe two of the many possible explanations for people's aggression and hatred. Which explanation makes the most sense to you? Why? What are the weaknesses of this approach?

14.2. Describe Kelly's concept of "cognitive simplicity". How might this characteristic impact one's ability to hate?

14.3. What are the three romantic attachment styles described by Shaver and colleagues? Briefly describe each. How are these similar to early attachment styles described by researchers such as Bowlby and Ainsworth?

14.4. How did Fromm's description of "love" differ from that of Freud? What would Fromm describe as immature love? Mature love?

14.5. How do Fromm's ideas of immature vs. mature love map onto Maslow's conceptions of B-love and D-love?

14.6. People who are androgynous (who are high on both masculinity and femininity) have been found to be least lonely. How might you explain this finding?

CHAPTER 15: WHERE WILL WE FIND PERSONALITY?

Multiple Choice Questions

15.1. Having the characteristic of "psychological mindedness"
  a. is predictive of a more mature adulthood
  b. means that one is likely a pretty good judge of what others feel
  c. means that someone is interested in the needs and experiences of others
  d. all of the above
  e. none of the above

ANSWER: D
DIFFICULTY LEVEL: M

15.2. An understanding of the needs, motives, feelings, and experiences of others
  a. is only available to psychologists and clergy
  b. depends on an innate skill that emerges in late childhood
  c. can be improved through study
  d. is correlated with a deficiency in self-understanding
  e. none of the above

ANSWER: C
DIFFICULTY LEVEL: M

15.3. People interested in the study of personality
  a. have historically included many immigrants, Jewish-Americans, and Catholic-Americans
  b. almost always have personality disorders themselves
  c. have often gone on to become dominant and powerful people in politics and the public arena
  d. have not traditionally been interested in introspection, preferring instead to study other people
  e. none of the above

ANSWER: A
DIFFICULTY LEVEL: C

15.4. Which of the following is NOT expected to significantly influence the way personality psychologists think about issues in the next century?
a. a better understanding of brain biochemistry
b. more accurate control of environmental contingencies
c. a decrease in the population of the planet
d. a better understanding of the genetic bases of personality
e. none of the above

ANSWER: C
DIFFICULTY LEVEL: M

15.5. Which of the following drugs was considered beneficial during Freud's era (and was taken by Freud himself), before its powerfully addictive nature was recognized?
a. cocaine
b. marijuana
c. peyote
d. LSD
e. snuff

ANSWER: A
DIFFICULTY LEVEL: M

15.6. Which well-known psychology professor at Harvard used, and advocated the use, of LSD during the 1960s?
a. Henry Murray
b. Cary Grant
c. Timothy Leary
d. Albert Bandura
e. Jane Loevinger

ANSWER: C
DIFFICULTY LEVEL: M

15.7. According to your textbook, personality may be studied from _____ basic perspectives.
a. three
b. four
c. five
d. eight
e. ten

ANSWER: D
DIFFICULTY LEVEL: E

15.8. Of the perspectives described in the textbook, which is the best?
a. the psychoanalytic
b. the behaviorist
c. the existentialist
d. the trait-based
e. none is "best"; instead each makes important contributions and has its own faults

ANSWER: E
DIFFICULTY LEVEL: E

15.9. Prozac blocks the reabsorption of ________ , and thereby affects mood.
a. dopamine
b. serotonin
c. oxygen
d. all of the above
e. none of the above

ANSWER: B
DIFFICULTY LEVEL: C

15.10. The drug Prozac (fluoxetine) was tested and originally approved for treating
a. depression
b. Attention Deficit Hyperactivity Disorder
c. anti-social personality disorder
d. schizophrenia
e. none of the above

ANSWER: A
DIFFICULTY LEVEL: C

15.11. The fact that altering brain chemistry can change behavior supports the following approach(es):
a. Cartesian dualism
b. behaviorist
c. interactionist
d. existential/humanistic
e. none of the above

ANSWER: E
DIFFICULTY LEVEL: C

15.12. Which of the following reflects a Skinnerian approach?
a. bonus pay as a reward for high volume sales
b. focus groups for individuals suffering from life-threatening illnesses
c. companies providing quiet rooms for self-reflection during the work day
d. all of the above
e. none of the above

ANSWER: A
DIFFICULTY LEVEL: M

15.13. Cartesian dualism describes the idea that
a. the mind and body are one integrated unit
b. individuals that have a propensity for violence can never be rehabilitated
c. the mind "dies" before the body does
d. the mind and body are separate entities
e. none of the above

ANSWER: D
DIFFICULTY LEVEL: M

15.14. How many basic perspectives of personality SHOULD there be
a. one
b. five
c. eight
d. ten
e. there is no correct number

ANSWER: E
DIFFICULTY LEVEL: C

15.15. People's deliberate use of psychoactive substances to influence behavior dates from
a. the beginnings of humankind
b. the ancient Greeks, who became skilled at making wine
c. the beginning of the 20th century, when recognition of the effects of alcohol led to the era of Prohibition
d. the middle of the 20th century, when chemical substances could first be synthesized from petroleum
e. the late 20th century, when advances in biotechnology allowed the creation of drugs specifically designed to affect neurotransmitter systems

ANSWER: A
DIFFICULTY LEVEL: M

Essay Questions

15.1. What is meant by the term "designer personality"? Do we have ways of creating anything close to this today? What are the advantages? Disadvantages?

15.2. What are the parallels between Skinner's ideas of utopia (in Walden Two) and many incentive plans instituted by large corporations today? Token economies found in classrooms?

15.3. Describe two positive potentialities of the human genome project, and one negative possibility.